The 30

SECRETS

of Happily Married Couples

The 30 SECRETS

of Happily Married Couples

DR. PAUL COLEMAN

BOB ADAMS, INC.
PUBLISHERS

Published by Bob Adams, Inc.
260 Center Street, Holbrook, MA 02343

ISBN: 1-55850-166-5

Printed in the United States of America

J I H G F E D C B A

This publication is designed to provide accurate and authoritative information with regard to the subject matter covered. It is sold with the understanding that the publisher is not engaged in rendering legal, accounting, or other professional advice. If legal advice or other expert assistance is required, the services of a qualified professional person should be sought.

— From a *Declaration of Principles* jointly adopted by a Committee of the American Bar Association and a Committee of Publishers and Associations.

Acknowledgments

A book such as this would not be possible if not for the dedicated work of many researchers in the field of marital therapy. In particular, I am most grateful for the research conducted by Dr. John Gottman and Dr. Howard Markman, whose work has inspired me.

Thanks again to my literary agent, Mike Snell, whose talent, enthusiasm, and bluefish paté are second to none.

Many thanks for the fine work by the editors at Bob Adams, Inc., notably Brandon Toropov and Kate Layzer.

To professors at Central Michigan University, especially Dr. Bill Hawkins, Dr. Carl Johnson, Dr. Sharon Bradley-Johnson, Dr. Dan King, Dr. Lynda King, and Dr. Ira Rosenbaum.

To my friend Dr. Foster Malmed, who never fails to crack me up.

To my longtime friends Norb and Gail Gottschling, Dr. Arnie Morgan and Alycia Morgan, Dr. Mike Leahy, and Deni O'Hara.

Of course, many thanks to my wife Jody for her love and encouragement.

And a special thanks to Luke, Anna, and Julia, who reminded me of my priorities when they insisted I read them a story instead of write.

For my parents,
George and Frances Coleman

Table of Contents

Read This First 9

1. Understanding The Ups And Downs of
   Changing 15

2. Knowing How to Talk 21

3. Minimizing Defensiveness 27

4. Knowing the Best Way to Read Minds 31

5. Putting Yourself in Your Partner's Shoes 35

6. Lowering Expectations (When It Comes to
   Raising Kids) 39

7. Balancing Logic and Emotion 43

8. Not Always Compromising 47

9. Not Withdrawing from Conflict or
   Conversation 51

10. Enjoying Time Together 57

11. Effective Problem Solving 63

12. Being a Cheerleader for Your Mate 69

13. Halting Arguments the Right Way 73

14. A Special Way of Caring 77

15. A Committed Relationship 83

16. Recognizing Your Role in a Problem. 87

17. Balancing Career and Family Roles. 93

18. Knowing You Can Trust. 99

19. Uncovering Hidden Agendas 105

20. Remaining Connected to Your Original
    Family. 111

21. Taking Time for Yourself 117

22. Knowing When to Keep Quiet—and When
    Not to 123

23. Loving It Up with Sex and Affection. 127

24. Keeping It Between the Two of You 133

25. Spiritual Beliefs and Shared Values 139

26. Holding Hands During Adversity 143

27. Knowing How (and When) to Forgive. 149

28. Being Positively Optimistic 155

29. Counting Your Blessings 161

30. Regular Progress Checks 165

    Notes 169

    Troubleshooter's Index 177

    Index 183

Read This First

Have you ever been to a restaurant and noticed (perhaps with envy and a bit of nostalgia) the one or two couples who seem just crazy about each other? Those romantics who devise ways to hold hands during the appetizer, lay bare their souls in intimate conversation over dinner, smile warmly and tenderly throughout the evening, and generally gaze upon one another with rapture?

Those were the days. Remember?

You don't have to be unhappy in your marriage to wish it could be happier. You can have a committed, caring relationship but still be weary of the complacency, frustrated with a partner's personality quirks, and secretly wondering, "Wouldn't it be wonderful if he'd only . . ."

You can have a good marriage but discover during times of stress and adversity that your relationship has its weak spots.

You can have a good marriage but still sense as you lie next to your partner at night a muted stirring of discontentment, a restlessness in your heart . . . a quiet realization that you're not as happy as you need to be and that some relationship changes are in order.

When you get right down to it, it isn't just better communication or more creative sex you want. It's ultimately marital happiness—marital joy—that you're seeking. And most of us want more because we deep-down believe that more joy is not only possible but necessary for a worthwhile life together.

So how do you transform a troubled relationship into a satisfying one? And how do you make a satisfactory marriage even happier? Answering those questions is what this book is all about.

Just How Happy Are We in Our Marriages?

Conventional Wisdom goofed.

It was commonly predicted, as the divorce rate rose in the seventies and eighties, that the average level of satisfaction for intact marriages would automatically improve, since the "unhappiest" couples had divorced and were no longer bringing down the overall average.

That prediction was wrong. In the past twenty years, measures of "happiness" in marriages have remained unchanged—and in some studies, declined slightly—despite the fact that the most unhappy couples have presumably divorced. What is going on in marriages with this thing called "happiness"?

In one of the best-designed studies of marital happiness, conducted by the Gallup organization in 1989, about 60 percent of the respondents rated their marriage as "very happy."[1] Yet of those "very happy" people, only 66 percent reported that their spouse respected their opinion. Only 64 percent of the "very happy" said their spouse made them feel important. Only 51 percent felt their spouse was romantic. When you add to these numbers the fact that almost 35 percent of couples rated their marriage as just "pretty happy," and that 37% of all women polled admitted there was a time when they were prepared to leave their husband, it becomes obvious that in the average American marriage, genuine happiness seems . . . blunted.

But so what. Is subdued marital happiness such a big deal? Absolutely. Dozens of research studies, several conducted by the National Opinion Research Center, have all concluded that the best predictor of overall happiness in life is marital happiness. (A happy marriage predicts overall happiness better than does job satisfaction, family life, friendships, finances, or good health.)[2] Happily married people live longer, have better adjusted children, and are healthier psychologically and physically. In one analysis of over eighteen thousand people from thirty-nine countries, women were happier than men, and married women were the happiest of all (followed by married men, unmarried women, and unmarried men).[3]

Do people strive and hope for more happiness in their marriage? Most couples report regular efforts to sustain and improve marital satisfaction. When asked in a Gallup Survey, "If you had to do it all over again, would you marry the same person?" 88 percent said "yes." But astoundingly, 26 percent of those "mostly dissatisfied" in their marriage also answered "yes," as did 23 percent of those "completely dissatisfied."[4] Clearly, many Americans (die-hard romantics?) don't want to give up when it comes to their marriage.

Does one's level of marital happiness predict who will eventually divorce? Not quite. It appears that those most happy are very unlikely to divorce, but many unhappy couples also remain together. Thus, a clear benefit to improving marital happiness is to reduce the risk of divorce in some cases and to improve the quality of family life for those couples who might remain together anyway.

Age and Happiness

In a poll conducted by the Massachusetts Mutual Life Insurance Company, 96 percent of respondents admitted that a primary goal in life was to get married and have a *happy* family life. But by now we are all familiar with the grim statistics. If you are currently married, the odds are 50 percent you've been separated or divorced, or are about to be. But did you know that *if you are between the ages of thirty-five and fifty-four, the odds increase to 67 percent,* according to the Gallup survey?

Researcher Lynn White at the University of Nebraska showed that because of fewer social barriers to divorce and more alternatives to current partners (especially available when you are younger), youthful couples don't have to be miserable in order to divorce. In other words, *today it requires higher levels of marital satisfaction to keep a couple together than in the days when divorce was not as socially acceptable.*[5] That is especially true if you are young.

What Makes a Happy Marriage Happy?

Is your spouse kind, trustworthy, gentle, a skilled lover, good with the kids, and helpful around the house? Having a spouse who fits that bill may seem ideal to some, yet these factors account for only 50 percent of happiness in a marriage.

Happiness is elusive. It is not a goal you can directly attain. Rather, it appears to be a by-product of living a caring, loving, moral, and accomplished life—and even then you can be unhappy from time to time. Certain events can make you feel happy (a birth of a child, a romantic anniversary gift, the bigger and better house or car) but it really is true that happiness in such cases is temporary. (A study of people who won large sums of money in the state lottery revealed that after one year the winners were not any happier than people of similar background and status who had not won money. In some ways, winners were less happy. They reported that common, mundane events they once enjoyed [eating a hearty breakfast, watching a favorite television show] were no longer satisfying.)[6]

How to Use This Book

This book is designed not just for the 6 percent of "not too happy" couples, but for the 94 percent of Americans who would classify their marriage as either "pretty happy" or as "very happy." Each chapter discusses one of thirty characteristics happy couples possess—and shows how you can develop or enhance those qualities too. Even in the best of marriages couples are sometimes at a loss to know what to do when an unexpected problem first develops or a troublesome issue recurs. And contented, loving couples occasionally welcome ideas that could help them boost their love and commitment toward one another. This is a book full of ideas, insights, exercises, and tips—founded on the latest research evidence—that can help you in your quest to make your marriage even happier.

The recommended exercises are not complicated and are designed to bring about rapid change (in a few hours to a few weeks). While many are designed for partners to perform together, most can be done without the cooperation of your spouse, although cooperation is very helpful. Some interventions will be more useful to your particular needs than other interventions. If you find the exercises or techniques aren't as effective as you'd hoped, consider the following:

- Have you applied the techniques properly and consistently?

- Are your expectations for change realistic? Most changes in behavior will be punctuated by backslides once in a while. And once positive changes do occur, developing them into habit requires additional effort. Marriages with very serious problems (alcoholism or other addictions, abusiveness, etc.) require specialized treatment in addition to marital therapy.

- Have you identified the real problem? (For example, sometimes a sexual problem is really a communication problem.

Sometimes stubbornness derives from a fear that one's feelings won't be taken seriously.)

● Have you or your partner sought the services of a divorce lawyer? If so, the marital problems are serious and commitment to the marriage is half-hearted at best. Talking with a qualified marital therapist will be a necessary step.

● Are other (non-marital) difficulties affecting you? If you or your mate is currently coping with a health, family, or career problem, the ability to deal effectively with the marriage may be compromised.

While this book is designed so that you can begin at any chapter you wish, I'd recommend you read chapters 1, 2, and 3 upon completing this one. These chapters provide you with a more realistic understanding of how couples can make relationship changes and will help you to communicate more effectively. Without effective communica-

---

Did You Know . . .

. . . that a happy marriage can profoundly affect your physical health? In one study, ten thousand Israeli men were evaluated to see who would develop angina pectoris—a condition where the blood supply to the heart is reduced. Amazingly, men who answered "YES" to the question "Does your wife show you her love?" were two times *less likely* to develop angina than men who responded "No."* (In other words, men whose hearts received less love from their wives were twice as likely to have hearts with a restricted blood supply, too.)

Researcher Janice Kiecolt-Glaser at Ohio State University School of Medicine measured the immune system functioning of married women. Immune functioning was better for women in satisfying marriages than for women in unsatisfying marriages (or for women recently separated or divorced.)#

No doubt about it, marital dissatisfaction increases one's odds of becoming physically ill.

* Medalie, J.H. & Goldbourt, H. Angina pectoris among 10,000 men: Psychosocial and other risk factors as evidenced by a multivariate analysis of a five year incidence study. *American Journal of Medicine, 60*, 910-921, 1976.

Kiecolt-Glaser, J.K., Fisher, L.D., Ogrocki, P., Stout, J.C., Speicher, C.E., & Glaser, R. Marital quality, marital disruption, and immune function. *Psychosomatic Medicine, 49*:13-34, 1987.

tion or realistic expectations, sincere attempts to improve marital happiness may fall short. Then select any chapter you think applies to your marriage and work from there. (For very specific concerns or issues, scan the "Troubleshooter's Index" at the end of the book.)

Making your marriage happier is far from impossible. In fact, I believe it is very possible to improve the quality and satisfaction of your relationship. Most of the material in this book is based on state-of-the art research on marital happiness, and the remainder is based upon my years of experience as a marriage and family therapist.

It's your marriage, your future, your happiness—and your family's happiness—that is at stake when you commit to a marriage. You and your family deserve to make your marriage the best it can be.

Secret #1

Understanding the Ups and Downs of Changing

Michelle and Dan didn't want a major overhaul of their marriage. They were committed to the relationship but a little impatient with one another. Progress in making minor improvements had gone into a skid recently, and each felt the other was being a tad uncooperative. All she wanted was for Dan to cut back on his overtime hours and to occasionally give the baby her three a.m. bottle. All he wanted was a little more lovemaking ("Since the baby was born we're down to once a fortnight. Isn't that below the national average?") and for her not to make their social plans without giving him a few days' notice.

"Before I see you next week," I said at the end of our meeting, "I'd like you to do something you may think a bit odd." Their curiosity piqued, I told them, "Between now and next time I'd like you to sleep on opposite sides of your bed, to switch positions. It's a small change, insignificant really, but I'm interested in any effects it may have."

The following week they reported the surprising results.

"I couldn't get comfortable at all," Michelle said. "On nights I was exhausted I'd fall into bed only to realize I had to switch sides."

"It didn't feel right to me either. In fact, last night we changed back. But interestingly, we made love three times this week. Something about being on a different side of the bed seemed more . . . provocative."

From that small exercise Michelle and Dan realized that even small changes can be awkward and that improvements in the marriage can come from unexpected places, if one remains open to the idea of change.

The Road to Improvement

Which attitude below do you think is realistic regarding efforts to improve one's marriage?

If a person really wants to change, willpower—not techniques—is all that's required.

The hardest part is getting started. Then it gets easier.

No one expects change overnight, but if significant progress isn't made within a few weeks, the person isn't trying hard enough.

If progress is followed by a reversal to old patterns of behaving, then the technique didn't really work.

If you answered "None of the above" you're correct. None is realistic. Let's look at each statement and see why.

If a person really wants to change, willpower—not techniques—is all that's required. All of us have heard of people who've changed bad habits without fuss or fanfare—they lost weight and kept it off with no fad dieting, or they stopped smoking "cold-turkey." But most people change their ways in fits and starts with a good deal of backsliding. Willpower is important, but without helpful strategies to stay on course, frustration and hopelessness can set in.

The hardest part is getting started. Then it gets easier. In my experience with couples, the hardest part about improving the relationship is not making changes. Rather, maintaining those changes is where couples need the most help. Sometimes partners set immediate goals too high—a setup for failure. Sometimes progress by one partner creates, paradoxically, anger in the other. "Yes, I know he's made improvements," one woman said, "but I keep thinking, 'It's too little too late.' Why didn't he change five years ago when I first asked him?" Sometimes positive changes result in unwanted side effects, such as when a couple with no leisure time together make more time—only to spend some of it arguing. Maintaining positive changes is very possible. People succeed in it every day. But it takes time and is often cumbersome. Without helpful guidelines, even spicing up your love life can leave you with a touch of indigestion.

No one expects change overnight, but if significant progress isn't made within a few weeks, the person isn't trying hard enough. What do we mean by "significant progress?" Some habits, like placing dirty clothes in a hamper instead of on the floor, can happen soon and are easy to monitor. Other changes, such as a "strong but silent" husband learning to disclose his feelings, can take time to develop and are not as easily monitored. (How can you tell if your mate is revealing *all* he's feeling?)

If progress is followed by a reversal to old patterns of behaving, then the technique didn't really work. Think again. The technique *did* work, but the new habit hasn't yet taken hold. When making relationship improvements, it's essential to understand that partners' actions mutually affect one another. If you take some improvements—yours or your mate's—for granted, the new changes will have less holding power because you've stopped encouraging them. As old patterns return, you and your partner can get critical and discouraged, which can add to your difficulties.

Realistically, improvements in marital happiness proceed like a bullish stock market. The trend over a week or a month is positive—gains are made—but some days show a decline. Care to take stock of your marriage?

What to Do

Follow the "Thirty Day Rule."[1] Give one another at least that long to make a noticeable (not necessarily an ideal) improvement. Abandoning efforts before thirty days reflects an unrealistic view of what the change process involves. If progress has been made by day thirty, keep at it. You're doing something right.

Appreciate changes by your spouse even if his or her heart isn't in it (yet). Changes in attitude often follow long after those in behavior. Typically, a spouse bent on improving her relationship wants two things from her husband: for him to make changes and for him to *want* to make changes. Consequently, when he agrees to certain requests, but grudgingly, she may respond, "Forget it. You have a lousy attitude." In happy marriages spouses occasionally do things they don't like—even grudgingly—to please their mates. When your partner pouts, tell him, "I know it isn't what you'd prefer, but it means a lot to me that you're doing it."

Minimize displays of impatience and criticism when progress seems slow. In a crisis, or after prolonged and repeated failures at improvement, many couples don't tolerate struggles to try harder. They want the problem *eliminated*. *Now.* Even patient partners can grow weary when progress is punctuated by slow-downs and setbacks.

At the first sign of mounting impatience, take a piece of paper, each of you, draw a line down the middle, and put your names on top—one on each side. Down the left-side column, mark the date. At the end of every day, each of you is to grade yourself and your partner on your efforts at improvement. For example, if you believe you did very well, give yourself an "A." If your partner was a bit less diligent, you might give her a "B+." However, there is to be *no discussion* about the grades for the next thirty days. This exercise provides you with important feedback from your mate without the added risk of an angry debate that might detour progress.

Predict obstacles to improvement. Ask yourself, "What could happen in the next few weeks that would slow me down or make me want to give up altogether?" Discuss your answers with your partner. Knowing in advance that a bad day at work, an illness, or spousal criticism can deter progress is good preventative planning.

Know what to say or do when you don't know what to say or do anymore. For example, if you find yourself faltering for no apparent reason, or if you can't find the right words to soothe a spouse frustrated by slow progress, say this: "I know I'm not doing my share and I'm sure you've noticed. I don't want this to be happening. Can you bear with me?" Or more generally, "I don't want to say or do the wrong thing but I'm not sure I'll succeed. Please don't take it personally." Such comments demonstrate an awareness of your difficulties, a sensitivity to your spouse's feelings, and a desire to improve. Consequently, your spouse may be supportive instead of critical.

Make goals as specific as possible. Wanting your spouse to "respect" you is too vague. Better to say, "I want you not to criticize me in front of company." One helpful guideline here is to imagine (it isn't hard) that your partner doesn't understand English very well. Vague requests like "more time together, more affection, more caring" are less clear than "I want us to go on a date twice a month" or "I want you to put your arm around me when we watch television" or "I'd like to play tennis once a week without you resenting it."

Keep in Mind:

- Don't minimize the small changes. They are the foundation for bigger ones.

- Understand that once changes have been made there is a tendency to relax, to "take your eye off the ball"—and for old patterns to re-emerge.

- Changing chronic ways of relating, especially if there is pressure to improve quickly, creates anxiety. It's uncomfortable but not fatal, and if it's not too intense it can spur on improvements rather than impede them.

- Nobody is perfect, and even irritating characteristics—however annoying—are part and parcel of the person you fell in love with.

Secret #2

Knowing How to Talk

"You know what would be really enjoyable?" Pam said excitedly to her husband Mark.

"Tell me," he answered slyly, eager to please.

"Since both of us don't go to work on Thursday mornings, wouldn't it be great if around 9:00 am we sat down, poured ourselves some coffee, and just talked for an hour? Mark? Honey, can you hear me? Mark, your eyes have glazed over again . . . ."

On average, wives enjoy talking with their mates more than husbands do. To women, the essence of any friendship is the ability to talk freely and disclose deep feelings. Men, however, rarely discuss their innermost feelings with their friends—wives included. Intimacy in male friendships shows up as good-natured teasing and "doing things together," such as playing racquetball or watching a ball game. Consequently, after an evening of television viewing with their wives, many husbands are surprised to hear their wives complain, "We don't do anything together anymore." (Men wonder: Doesn't watching "Star Trek" count for something?)

"I Think We Should Talk about How We Don't Talk Anymore"
Intimacy is at its highest with your partner—no, not when you're making love, but when you're disclosing feelings. Even communicating your ideas on mundane issues is a good way to increase a sense of partnership. Talking isn't difficult. But communicating effectively can take practice. Why is communication the number-one concern of distressed couples? How do efforts to have a simple dialogue get bogged down? Three reasons predominate.

1. *Conflicting expectations.* According to author Deborah Tannen,[1] being able to talk things out is a sign to most women that the relationship is working. But to men, the relationship is not working well if you have to keep talking about it. The key is expectations. Couples who rarely talk beyond superficial matters but never expect more are not dissatisfied. But in the 1990s, few people enter a relationship expecting little conversation. In fact, a 1989 report in the journal *Sex Roles* showed that marital satisfaction for 192 rural Alabama couples was best predicted by the husband's expressiveness.[2] The more warmth, sensitivity, and emotional expression the husbands conveyed, the happier the marriages.

2. *The mechanics of conversation.* For effective dialogue, the speaker must first say what he means. "I'm upset" is vague. It can mean anything from "I'm annoyed" to "I'm furious." "Let's go out for dinner tonight" might imply "You arrange for a babysitter and I'll make the dinner reservations." Do you know what your mate means when she says, "I'm tired"? Is she stating a fact or is she making a request? ("I'm tired . . . So would you watch the kids for a while?")

   If a speaker successfully says what he means, does the listener hear the message accurately? When Ken said, "Let's go to a movie this weekend," Sarah was annoyed. She heard Ken's remark as a *demand* ("We are going to the movies") when in fact he expressed a *desire* and was quite willing to negotiate.

   Conversations also get complicated when non-verbal expressions (e.g., a bored look) don't match the spoken words ("I'm having a great time at this party.") As a general rule, when there is an inconsistency between verbal and non-verbal expressions, people view the non-verbal signs as a true reflection of how someone is feeling. Unfortunately, according to researchers Patricia Noller and Mary Anne Fitzpatrick, men are better at decoding the non-verbal messages of strangers than those of their wives.[3] And men's decoding skills worsen when their wives are distressed. It appears that a husband's anxiety increases when his wife is unhappy, and his anxiety impairs his ability to understand her non-verbal messages.

3. *The environment.* Trying to talk effectively when the kids are raising a ruckus, the radio is blaring, or when you are about to leave for work increases the chances for miscommunication. Reducing distractions is necessary, especially for important discussions.

What to Do

Practice reflective listening. Ideally, practice it three to five times a week for at least twenty minutes each time. This time-honored technique has three basic steps:

1. Partner A speaks until a complete thought has been expressed (it should not take longer than twenty to thirty seconds to complete one thought).

2. Partner B *summarizes* or *paraphrases* what was just heard. *It is essential that Partner B not agree, disagree, debate, or otherwise challenge Partner A.* This is simply the opportunity for Partner B to express his understanding of what was just said. Preface summary statements with the phrase, "What you are saying is . . ." or "I hear you telling me that . . ." Simply stating "I understand what you're saying" is *not* enough.

3. Partner A acknowledges that B's summary was accurate and continues speaking (guided by step one) until her point of view was fully expressed and understood. If Partner A does not believe that B's summary is accurate, she repeats her point in a slightly different way and allows B the opportunity to summarize it again. That pattern continues until A feels completely understood by B. Then it is B's turn to speak while A practices reflective listening.

Effective use of reflective listening improves understanding and drastically reduces angry interruptions and no-win debates.

Agree to have a one-sided conversation. If hostility is high and impedes your ability to use reflective listening, agree to take fifteen minutes a day to deal with a high-conflict issue. Divide the time—seven minutes each with a one-minute break. When one speaks the other listens quietly and *does not even summarize or paraphrase. No discus-*

sion of the topic is to occur in any other context.[4] Do this daily for at least one week before attempting reflective listening. This prevents partners from sandbagging one another by bringing up a hot topic at an inconvenient time. It eliminates hostile exchanges and allows each partner to explore in-depth his or her concerns about the issue and to hear a partner's concerns fully.

Validate a partner's comments. Comments are validated not when you agree with them but when you can say, "Given your perception of events, your ideas on what to do make sense" or "Given your interpretations, I don't blame you for feeling the way you do." Most people believe their reactions make perfect sense. Having a different point of view is not divisive. Expressing it in a manner that conveys, "You are foolish to feel the way you do," is. If you can't validate your partner's comments, then you don't fully understand them. Try reflective listening again.

Don't offer advice or solutions to problems unless explicitly asked (husbands, especially, take heed). There are two kinds of communication: expression of one's feelings and thoughts, and problem-solving. Often, one partner's wish to blow off steam—to express feelings about a hard day—is interpreted by the other as an invitation to problem-solve. Husbands in particular have a difficult time listening to their wives discuss personal problems without trying to solve the problems. Many wives resent that. This pattern also occurs when one partner simply expresses a wish and the other responds to it as if it were a topic for negotiation (a problem to be solved):

"Wouldn't it be great if we had a boat?"

"A boat? You know we can't afford a boat."

"I wasn't saying we should buy one, I was just saying it would be nice if we had one."

"No use talking about something we won't get."

Learn to recognize which kind of communication is needed (expression of feelings or problem-solving), and you won't miss the boat when it comes to constructive dialogue.

Write two letters to clear up confusion and improve mutual understanding: a letter to your partner stating your point of view and a letter to yourself stating your partner's point of view.[5] A thoughtful, sincere letter can halt uncooperative dialogues and convey understanding better than some verbal exchanges. Eventually, successful letter writing leads to successful verbal dialogue, since each partner is now more willing to listen and give his or her mate the benefit of the doubt.

Keep in Mind

- Discussing differences with your mate may yield short-term distress (an argument, physical discomfort, brooding) but pays long-term dividends.

- Expect complications if your non-verbal messages clash with your verbal messages.

- Reflective listening requires more practice than you think. Every time an argument develops, you can bet there was no attempt at reflective listening.

- When discussions go nowhere, one or both of you is missing something important. Aim for mutual understanding, not winning the argument or being right.

Did You Know...

... that interrupting your mate may not always hinder communication? A 1981 study revealed that happy couples interrupted one another 150 percent more often than unhappy couples.* Apparently, "simultaneous speech" (as it was termed by the researchers) is not necessarily a no-no. One hypothesis for that finding is that interruptions per se don't clog communication and fuel fights. It depends on the meaning given the interruption. Unhappy couples construe interruptions as demonstrating rudeness and disrespect. Happy couples view interruptions by their mates as signs of interest in what is being discussed. So if you want to interrupt your mate, go ahead. But your relationship had better be a happy one.

* Margolin, G. & Wampold, B.E. Sequential analysis of conflict and accord in distressed and nondistressed marital partners. *Journal of Consulting and Clinical Psychology, 49,* 1981, 554-567.

Secret #3

Minimizing Defensiveness

"I hate it when you get so mad, Charlie. Why can't I tell you my concerns about our relationship without you getting irate?"

"I get mad because you make me mad, Karla."

"Oh, it's my fault, is that it? When will you take responsibility for your own actions?"

"I do take responsibility. Oh, forget it. You just don't understand."

Charlie and Karla talked like that a lot of the time, which is why they eventually ended their relationship. Their main difficulty was that their discussions—punctuated by name-calling and accusations—led to defensiveness, and defensiveness squeezed the breath out of any intimate dialogue.

Defensiveness is quite common. We show defensiveness when we make excuses for our behavior or attack another's viewpoint. A defensive person is quick to feel accused. But often, when defensiveness causes a conversation to break down, the person *was* being accused. Badgering your mate also increases his stubbornness and defensiveness. So does making frequent criticisms. An easy formula to remember is this: Accusations + Badgering + Criticisms = Defensiveness.

Do your conversations result in defensiveness? If so, matters won't likely improve without intervention. One study, in which couples' communication styles were examined over a five-year period, showed that the patterns of interaction didn't change much during that time.[1]

Psychologists have found that increasing positive interactions (such as being polite, respectful, and considerate) can improve marital quality, but reducing defensiveness and negative interactions is more vital.[2] Esteemed psychologist John Gottman reported that in a distressed marriage, one destructive or hurtful interaction can often wipe away the effects of ten positive and constructive interactions.[3]

Some actions are easy to identify as being destructive: physical abuse, yelling, put-downs, cruel remarks—they poison a relationship and are not easily forgotten. But partners in solid relationships are often surprised at how defensive their mate can be even when no accusations were made. Are there subtle ways to promote defensiveness? Yes. Researchers Jacqueline Schachter and Dan O'Leary studied whether the *intent* of one spouse's message matched the *impact* it had on the mate.[4] It seemed that most people rated the *intent* of their message as more positive than did the spouse who received the message. That was true whether the couples were classified as happy or unhappy. (When spouses knew they were sending a negative message, their partners still interpreted the message more negatively than was intended.) This discrepancy between *intent* and *impact* was less troublesome for happy couples because most of their messages were very positive, overall. But that helps explain why some spouses—who think they are making positive or neutral comments—might provoke defensiveness in their mate.

What to Do

Make A-B-C statements. Instead of accusing, phrase your concerns this way: "When I see (or hear) you do A, I think B and respond C." Example: "When I wait for you while you're talking on the phone for an hour, I think you don't care about my feelings and I resent it." That is more clear and less accusatory than the shotgun style of "You don't care about my feelings." A-B-C statements begin with "I" ("When I hear you yelling . . .") and not "You" ("When *you* are yelling . . ."). Comments that begin with "You" automatically promote defensiveness.

Use Intent-Impact cards.[5] Remove the hearts and clubs from a deck of playing cards and divide them equally between you and your spouse. Now begin a conversation, speaking one at a time. Every time you believe you are saying something in a positive way, give your partner a heart card. If you believe you are being more negative, hand out a club card. As the listener, whenever you believe your mate is speaking in a positive way, hand over a heart card. If negative, hand over a club card. This exercise does two things. At a minimum it slows down the conversation, which prevents rapid escalations of negativity. More importantly, it clarifies what a speaker's INTENT is and what the IMPACT is on the receiver. Partners often believe they are revealing more positiveness and therefore can't understand when their mates react with hostility to a "perfectly nice comment."

Since many arguments erupt unplanned, it's helpful to agree that the next time an argument occurs one of you will call "Time-Out." Then you can continue the discussion using the cards.

If you must make a complaint, write it out first. Your partner is to read it without comment and then the two of you can discuss it at least half an hour later. (Try writing it in the A-B-C format). This prevents unfortunate, off-the-cuff reactions to the complaint while allowing for a thoughtful response.

If you must make a complaint, check first to see whether you've overlooked something positive about your mate. Criticisms are never appreciated when the criticized spouse is expecting a compliment. Dave complained to Sue that she ignored his mother when his parents visited. Sue got angry. She had expected him to compliment her for the feast she had prepared and for "going out of my way" to be cordial. Dave missed both an opportunity to express gratitude and an opportunity for his complaint to be taken seriously.

If you're very angry with your mate, don't ask "Why?" questions. "Why did you arrive home now instead of an hour ago?" "I saw you looking at that woman that way. Why did you do that?" "Why don't you send me flowers anymore?" Asking such questions invites your partner to come up with some explanation—when no explanation will be good enough. Instead, better to make a comment (not a question) followed by a specific request. "I like it when you surprise me with gifts. Do you think you could surprise me sometime soon?"

If you must know a reason, better to say "Please help me understand why . . ." It's less provocative and demonstrates that you haven't yet passed judgment on his behavior.

If your mate makes an angry complaint that is farfetched or downright false, avoid being argumentative or righteously indignant.[6] Better to say, "I don't understand what you are saying. Could you say it another way and help me make sense of it?" This demonstrates patience, prevents a debate on semantics ("How can you say I *never* care about your feelings, I've cared about your feelings plenty of times . . ."), and gives your mate an opportunity to rethink and rephrase what he really means.

Bail out. If your dialogue is promoting defensiveness despite best attempts to do otherwise, halt the conversation and ask your spouse, "What could I say or do right now that would help you to feel better understood?" That prevents escalations of defensiveness, shows consideration, and indicates your strong desire to really make the discussion work *for* the relationship, not *against* it.

Keep in Mind

- Accusations, badgering, and criticisms are the perfect ingredients for defensiveness.

- You may intend to say something in a positive or neutral way, but your mate may interpret it a bit less positively. That's not uncommon.

- Name-calling, abusiveness, and put-downs will close off your partner's heart more quickly than anything else you can do.

- Your anger may be legitimate, but expressing it in a hostile manner rarely gets you what you want.

- It's possible to make a complaint without being accusatory or insensitive. The key is to not pass judgment or label your partner but rather to state clearly what your perceptions are and offer suggestions on how you'd like him or her to act differently.

Secret #4

Knowing the Best Way to Read Minds

Happy couples do it just as often as unhappy couples, but they do it better.

It's called *mind reading* and it has a public relations problem. The best marriage therapists and communication experts warn of the dangers of mind reading while happy couples do it often with no adverse effects. Mind reading is as it sounds: assuming you know what really is going on in your spouse's head without asking him.

The following are examples of mind reading:

"I knew you'd like a sandwich for lunch so I made you one."

"You're lying."

"You would rather watch television than spend time alone with me."

"You're preoccupied. What's wrong?"

"Admit it. You're jealous."

"You haven't wanted to have sex in three weeks. You're avoiding me."

"Let's skip dessert. You only ate half of your meal so you must not be hungry."

In all of the above examples, the speaker presumed to know the listener's thoughts and feelings—without bothering to ask.

Another common form of mind reading occurs when one spouse speaks for another spouse. Example: "Yes, mother. Joe and I would love to come for dinner tonight." Here, the woman spoke for her husband without checking with him.

Mind reading is sometimes glorified as romantic ("We know each other so well [giggle] we even finish each other's sentences!"[swoon]). To others, it is a subtle indication of love and caring ("If you loved me, you'd know what I want without my having to tell you.") Most partners eventually come to believe that they know their spouse only too well and that their mind reading skill is well-honed. But they are mistaken. The less happy they are in their marriage, *the less adept they are at mind reading.* Dissatisfied partners misunderstand one another more often than they realize. One reason? People tend to seek out and interpret events in a manner that maintains pre-existing beliefs.[1] So if they believe their spouse is inconsiderate, they'll see evidence of that more than evidence to the contrary.

In the best of relationships, mind reading occurs without much exasperation—not because the mind reader is necessarily correct but because his or her accompanying emotion is positive or, at least, neutral. Therapist and researcher John Gottman discovered that mind reading is not tolerated well in unhappy marriages because the emotion accompanying the mind reading is usually negative (anger or disgust).[2] Consequently, mind reading is viewed as a hostile, intrusive act. Happy couples view mind reading as a neutral "feeling probe," an attempt by a partner to gently ascertain what the other is thinking or feeling.

So a happy spouse might respond to the comment "I knew you'd like a sandwich for lunch so I made you one" in one of these ways:

"Great. Thanks."

"Actually, I was planning on eating something else, but the sandwich will do fine. Thanks."

"Actually, I had my heart set on that leftover turkey soup. I'll wrap up the sandwich for another time. Thanks anyway."

An unhappy spouse might respond to the same sandwich offer this way:

"Why don't you ask me what I want first? How do you know I want a sandwich?"

So, mind read if you wish, but if your marriage needs improving, it's best to approach it with some positive emotion.

What to Do

Turn your mind reading comment from a statement into a question. "I know you don't want to go skiing with me" then becomes "I know you don't want to go skiing with me. Or do you?" The goal is to ask a question that checks-out your mate's thoughts and feelings. Another way to transform a mind reading statement into a question: "You would rather watch television than spend time with me. Do I have that right?"

If you must mind read, do so, but admit you are doing so.
    "You're only putting the baby to sleep earlier because you want to have sex with me." To that statement add "I know I'm mind reading and I know that annoys you." He may not like what you are saying (regarding the baby) but at least you can discuss the issue at hand without getting sidetracked by his accusing you of mind reading.

Qualify your remarks. Preface your mind reading comment with phrases like "It seems to me that . . ." or "Sometimes I wonder if . . ." or "Could it be that . . . ." Doing so conveys a tentativeness that might be appreciated.

Keep in Mind
- Mind reading per se is not a romantic indication of one's depth of love. But how you phrase your mind reading comment, or how you respond to such a comment, is.

Did You Know . . .

. . . that your level of marital satisfaction can determine whether you see your partner's strengths or only her weaknesses?

    In one study, happy and unhappy couples were asked to discuss an area of conflict.* But one of the pair was secretly asked by the researcher to be especially "positive" or "negative" during the discussion. Later, the unsuspecting spouses were asked why they believed their spouse was so positive or negative. Spouses in happy marriages viewed their mates' negativity caused by extenuating events ("She must not be feeling well") while spouses in unhappy marriages viewed their mates' negativity as a stable character flaw ("She's always like that"). Unhappy partners regarded their mates' positive remarks as the result of extenuating circumstances ("He must be in a good mood today") rather than as a consequence of their personality.

    The moral? The happier you are, the more you'll give your partner the benefit of the doubt. The unhappier you are, the more you'll doubt your partner's benefits.

* Jacobsen, N.S., Follette, V., & McDonald, D. Reactivity to positive and negative behavior in distressed and nondistressed married couples. *Journal of Consulting and Clinical Psychology* 1982, *50*, 706-714.

- A person's last refuge for solitude and solace is his or her mind. Even if your mind reading efforts are a positive "feeling-probe," your mate might still regard it as an intrusion. Respect your partner's privacy as often as you can.

- If you're dissatisfied, you won't mind read very accurately (although you'll be convinced you are accurate).

Putting Yourself in Your Partner's Shoes

When Janet heard Jack yelling at the kids again she stormed into the room. "I've told you to be calmer with the boys, Jack, but still you yell. Don't you realize how your harshness makes them, and me, feel?"

"Of course I know how everyone feels," Jack responded angrily. "You feel I'm being mean and insensitive. God knows you've told me a hundred times."

Jack understood Janet's feelings but he had no empathy for them. He didn't fully grasp what it was like to be in her shoes. For that matter, Janet had no empathy for Jack.

Understanding without empathy is like a fancy car low on gasoline. It looks nice and has great potential, but it won't take you very far.

What Is Empathy?

It was almost dinner time. The spaghetti was boiling over, the baby was fussy, and Ted was surprised to see his wife curled up in a chair reading her favorite magazine. At first he was irritated. Then he thought, *I know how it feels to want to escape during hectic times. Maybe she wanted just a few minutes of solitude before gearing up for dinner. I'll go tend the spaghetti and let her finish the article.*

That's empathy.

Psychologist Michael Nichols of Albany Medical College says that empathy has two essential ingredients: understanding *plus* acceptance.[1] In the above example, Ted demonstrated both. He understood his wife's need for some quiet time *and* he accepted it. He didn't criticize her or try to get her to change. In other words, what she did was okay. (Inconvenient, but okay.)

When couples go round and round on some issue, each may spout the words, "I understand what you're saying, *but* . . .". They may or may not truly understand. However, saying *"but"* indicates *they don't accept* their partner's having those thoughts and feelings. When spouses, polarized over some issue, stubbornly dig in their heels during an argument, you can bet one of two things is happening: they believe their partner misunderstands, or they believe their partner understands but doesn't care.

Understanding plus acceptance is essential if you want to show you care.

Empathy is harder to come by during an argument. It's difficult to show understanding and acceptance if you believe you aren't receiving any. Commonly, spouses feel more empathy for each other when they are alone and thinking about their mate. For example, the guilty feeling one gets when driving to work after an argument often derives from empathy. Now that you have time to sort through matters, you realize you were a bit unfair or critical—and you imagine how your spouse must be feeling.

Do you spend much time and energy *repeatedly* trying to get your partner to change his ways? If so, you aren't showing empathy (neither, probably, is your mate). If he doesn't believe you understand his point of view and accept his feelings, he'll resist your efforts to change him. Wouldn't you? (If you answered "Yes," you score a point for being empathic.)

To accept your partner's feelings and habits doesn't mean you must like them, agree with them, or not make requests for change. It means you won't reject your partner for having them. It means they make some sense when you look at the bigger picture.

Here is an example of showing empathy while still making a request for change:

It was Sam's second marriage. He believed his first wife took advantage of him financially—leaving him virtually bankrupt—and now he wanted Linda to understand why he should put her on an allowance. Linda didn't care for the idea.

"I know Margie really did waste your money," Linda said. "And you've worked so hard to get out of debt. I guess I can't blame you for wanting to put me on an allowance. But at the same time I want you to believe you can trust me not to do what Margie did to you. How can I earn your trust if you restrict my spending?"

"You're saying that you want me to believe in you without having to restrict you, is that right?" Sam asked.

"Yes," Linda answered. "But I know I'm asking a lot after what you went through with Margie."

Linda very effectively entered into Sam's world—she tried to view the issue as Sam viewed it, used his assumptions, and recognized his right to feel the way he did. Consequently, Sam not only felt more understood, he felt more relaxed and loved. When you want to assess whether you've spoken empathically, look for signs that your mate feels relieved, reassured, and calmed.

What to Do

Think about your spouse and ask yourself, "What must it be like for her to have me around right now?" Review things you've said or done during the day—even mundane things—and try to imagine how she might have felt about them.

Is it possible you stepped on your partner's feelings during the day without realizing it? Better to ask about it now. Even if you weren't insensitive, your mate will appreciate your thoughtfulness in asking.

Despite your partner's bad mood or irritating habits, imagine that deep down he or she is feeling lonely. How might the loneliness have developed? Might your partner be feeling lonely right this minute (even if he or she appears otherwise)? A person feels lonely when an important part of them can't be understood, accepted, or shared.

Create "emotional word-pictures" to help your mate empathize with you.[2] Emotional word-pictures are graphic memories of something your mate experienced that are similar to something you are now experiencing. ("Remember how you felt when you discovered I bounced a check? Well, I feel similarly when . . .") There are three steps to developing emotional word-pictures. First, identify the feeling you want your mate to understand and accept (such as lonely, hurt, excited, inadequate, furious, betrayed, sexy, etc.). Second, recall an experience in your mate's life when you believe he felt the same. The more emotional the experience was for him, the better. Third, refresh his memory. Be as graphic as possible ("Remember the promotion you missed out on, the one you worked so hard to try to get? Remember when you came home that day and felt like quitting? Well, I feel similarly about . . . .") If your mate was able to recall strong feelings, he'll more likely empathize with you.

Exchange roles. Select any topic and begin expressing the viewpoint you believe your partner holds. Your mate should do the same. If you can't express your partner's views accurately, call a time-out and have your spouse reiterate her position. Then try reversing roles again. To add a dose of realism, sit in a chair your mate usually occupies, or sit on the side of the bed your partner sleeps on.

Think of one or two things your spouse has told you (many, many times) that she enjoys or needs but that rarely come about easily. For example, you may know she prefers to have twenty minutes to settle in after arriving home from work, but it's usually too hectic to accommodate her. Or, he might prefer that the house be tidied up before going to bed, but both of you are too tired to do it. Maybe your spouse would like to have ten soothing minutes of music and decaffeinated coffee after dinner, but bath time for the kids often interferes. Once a week, give your partner that special gift without him having to ask. It's a small gesture but one loaded with meaning, since your mate will feel cared for and empathized with.

Keep in Mind

- To be empathic, you must temporarily suspend your beliefs about what is right or wrong, appropriate or inappropriate.

- Understanding must precede empathy.

- Empathy is rare in the heat of conflict. A cooler climate, plus time to sort through feelings, often helps.

Secret #6

Lowering Expectations
(WHEN IT COMES TO RAISING KIDS)

You be the psychologist. Imagine that a husband or wife calls you on the phone and describes their marriage this way:

- We argue more than we used to.

- We seem to want more solitary time, away from each other.

- When we do spend time together, we talk about bills or the house—rarely do we have fun anymore.

- Our sex life has deteriorated.

- We're both more irritable, more tired.

- We worry more than we used to.

What's your diagnosis, doctor? Is this a marriage in serious trouble? Possibly. But all of the above accurately describes one kind of special relationship: a couple with small children.

THE KID FACTOR

Having children changes forever the face of the marital relationship. When you ask elderly couples what was most meaningful in their lives, most will tell you it was raising their children. Most will say children made their lives fulfilling and worth living. But when you measure marital happiness on a day-in, day-out basis, the evidence is overwhelming: couples with children are less happy than childless couples. That is true regardless of age, sex, years of education, religion, race, or income.[1]

One 1985 study showed that marital satisfaction declined within the first six months of a child's life, especially for mothers.[2] By eighteen months, satisfaction had declined for fathers and *never recovered* until the children left home. Certainly couples with children vary a great deal on their level of happiness, but in general, happiness dips once children arrive. Marital happiness peaks between the honeymoon and the birth of the first child. It reaches a second peak after the children have left the homestead. Evidently, the "empty nest syndrome"— the difficulty parents have adjusting to a childless home—has been overrated. For the majority of couples, marital happiness usually improves when the children grow up and get out. (For men, that is the happiest time of their lives.)

While the hassles and financial burden of raising children can contribute to dissatisfaction, the main reason for lower satisfaction among couples with children is this: these couples have less time to talk to one another and less leisure time to enjoy together.[3] The couples hardest hit are those with unrealistic expectations of life with children. "I truly believed that having a child meant lullabies, cooing in a rocking chair, and constant 'oohs' and 'ahs' from family and friends. My mother 'oohs,' but I still change the diaper. I can't hear the lullabies for all the crying, and my husband is too tired to do much of anything. And who has time to sit in a goddamned rocking chair?"

Despite abundant evidence that the presence of children reduces marital happiness, most people believe otherwise. The belief that childless couples will have empty and unfulfilling lives was widespread, according to a 1977 Gallup survey.[4] This "parenthood paradox"—the appeal of being a parent despite the fact that it reduces overall happiness—may have an explanation, according to social psychologist Roy Baumeister.[5] Children are a powerful source of meaning and purpose for parents. Raising children requires sacrifice and commitment. Parents must care for a child's immediate needs (food, clothes, shelter, first aid), short-term needs (helping them adjust to school or a new baby sister), and long-term needs (education, social and moral development). All things considered, according to Baumeister "parenthood may be a poor strategy for finding happiness but an excellent one for achieving a meaningful life."[6]

Are you one of those people who believed life would be complete once you had children? Then, despite some happy days, you are probably a tad disenchanted if you do have kids. But improved happiness is still possible to achieve.

What to Do

Make a list of all the enjoyable things you've cut back on since you've had children. Include solitary activities (such as exercising, listening to music) and couple activities (sex, taking walks, going out to dinner, etc.) Plan that at least once a week you'll do one thing each from your list of solitary and marital activities. You'll feel less irritable, more relaxed, and will probably enjoy the time with the children more.

Write it down. Attach a sheet of paper to the refrigerator and make a list of all the child-related activities you do during the course of the day. (Write each item down after you've done it.) Your partner should do the same. One spouse will probably outperform the other, but that is often acceptable. (Most couples make allowances for such things as who works more hours at the office, who is better at some tasks than others, etc.) Exchange lists. Carefully review all your partner has written. Select one or two items that you find most helpful or meaningful or that you appreciate, and tell your partner. Gratitude and empathy for your spouse's child-care activities improves intimacy.

Examine your list and discuss potential changes with your partner. (Please be sure you've already made progress on the communication exercises in chapter 2.) For example, you may discover that, while

---

Did You Know . . .

. . . that couples with only one child, a boy, are 9 percent less likely to divorce than if the child were a girl?* And couples with two children, both boys, are 18 percent less likely to divorce than couples with only two girls? Evidently, fathers spend more time in child-care activities with sons than with daughters. A father's greater involvement in child-care usually improves marital satisfaction and reduces the risk of separation and divorce.

A 1991 study supported the claim that fathers spend more time with their sons, but found that if a girl had brothers, her father's involvement in her life was much greater than if she had no brothers.[#]

---

*Morgan, S.P., Lye, D.N. and Condran, G.A. Sons, daughters, and the risk of marital disruption *American Journal of Sociology, 94*, 1988, 110-129.

[#] Harris, Kathleen & Morgan, S Philip. Fathers, sons, and daughters: differential paternal involvement in parenting. *Journal of Marriage and the Family, 53*, 1991, 531-544.

each of you plays with the children a reasonable amount of time, there is little individual attention paid to each child in play. Or you may discover that some household chores routinely prevent one partner from enjoying family time. Consequently, letting husbands take the kids to the playground while wives mow the lawn may be a pleasant change of pace. If dad routinely gives the kids their breakfast and mom routinely puts them to bed, switching jobs on occasion may be a nice idea.

Complete the following sentence: Just for today, I'd like to do less of _____ *and more of* _____. Making a small, time-limited change in your daily routine can decrease frustration with role demands.

Remind yourself daily (place a note on your refrigerator or your dresser) that there is positive value to your role as a parent. Research shows that parents "are quite willing to tolerate unpleasant emotions and feelings, as long as the overall pattern seems favorable to them and . . . bad emotions are thus regarded as individual, isolated fragments, none of which can compare with the broad pattern of positive emotions and valuable progress."[7] Emphasize the positive, meaningful consequences of parenthood and pat yourself on the back for all of your efforts to be a loving, committed parent.

Keep in Mind

- A parent's "presence," not their "presents" usually means more to a child.[8]

- Even in "non-traditional" marriages, the presence of children often results in a shift toward more traditional roles.[9]

- The presence of your children allows you to know your parents and siblings in a new way. It can be enjoyable relating to your brother now that he's "Uncle" and your Dad now that he's "Grampa."

Secret #7

Balancing Logic and Emotion

"Dan, Jennifer is on the phone. Her grades were poor this semester and she's thinking of quitting school. Would you talk to her and put some sense into that girl?"

"I'll speak with her, Mary" Dan answered, "but she's twenty and old enough to make her own decisions."

"But this is school—her future—that's at stake! How can you be so casual?"

"Mary, I've told you before that if Jenny quits school she'll just have to get a job. If she regrets her decision later then she can reapply to college. Simple."

"Sometimes I just don't think you care, Dan," Mary concluded.

Dan and Mary could have been discussing any topic—money, vacation plans, Mary's career—and the style of the conversation would be the same. Mary would be emotional about something and Dan would approach the topic like a machine (chock full of computer chips, but no heart). It wasn't differences in opinion that divided them. In the above example, Mary actually agreed with Dan that Jennifer was old enough to make her own decisions. What really bothered Mary was Jim's logical, "just the facts, Ma'am," stance. And Jim was troubled by Mary's "the sky is falling" stance. Yes, he was concerned about Jennifer, but he believed his feelings had little to do with the problem at hand. So why bother bringing up feelings?

They had other differences, too. Mary liked spontaneity, Dan followed an itinerary. Mary enjoyed idle chats and meandering, unfocused discussions. Dan liked to "get to the point." To Mary, expressing feelings was one way of being intimate. To Dan, feelings were problems to be solved.

The Head or The Heart? Which Makes Better Sense?

As you might guess, both reason and emotion must be balanced for healthy living. Actually, if Dan and Mary could be merged into one person, that person would be balanced. But as it is, Mary could bone up on Logic 101, and Dan, well, he could benefit from a good cry. (He won't agree, though.)

What Dan and Mary often forget is that the very traits that annoy them now were what first attracted them to their partner. In the early days Dan was captivated by Mary's sentimentality, her warmth and intimacy. Now, he regards her as too emotional and clingy, demanding affection without appropriate restraint. In the early days Mary was entranced by Dan's strong and silent ways. He always seemed in control, stable, and secure. Now, he seems cold. Unfeeling. An old poop. What went wrong?

Mary did have a logical side to her personality, but it made her uneasy. Making logical decisions that trampled someone's feelings seemed wrong. She would rather be liked than make an unfair decision. Dan had an emotional side but it made him uncomfortable. Expressing feelings was a bit unmanly and tended to pop the cork from his tightly controlled demeanor. So each allowed that hidden part of themselves to be expressed by their partner.

In one U.C.L.A. study of fifty-five couples, many opposing personality patterns emerged. Some partners were assertive, their mates unassertive. Some were flirtatious, their mates jealous. But one of the patterns most associated with satisfaction was this: if, during an argument, one partner was emotional while the other was logical, that relationship was unsatisfying.[1]

Having opposing styles as Dan and Mary do is common, though sometimes troubling. A personality transformation won't happen soon, but steps can be taken so that the differences between you and your mate don't have to make a difference.

What to Do

Watch your phrasing. If you must approach a problem analytically, be sure to mention to your mate what "worries" or "concerns" you about the matter. You don't have to abandon logic to admit feelings. Using the example at the beginning of this chapter, if Dan admitted to Mary that his daughter's intention to quit school *worried* him, Mary wouldn't regard him as unfeeling. (Women in particular are responsive to disclosure of a mate's feelings.)

When you're being very emotional or very logical, admit it. Tell your spouse, "I'm aware I'm being very analytical (or emotional) now, and I know that bothers you." That shows consideration and may halt an escalating argument. (By the way, "highly emotional" spouses often see the logic of matters if you respond sensitively to their feelings. "Overly logical" spouse often "open up" their feelings when they feel respected and the pressure is off.)

Make a list of all the benefits/advantages of having an emotional or logical spouse.[2] For example, he may have a hard time showing his feelings, but he's probably dependable, a hard worker, and well organized. She may let her emotions run her life, but she provides the warmth and friendship you need. Review the list several times daily for at least a week. It will help you keep a balanced perspective.

Force yourself to comment on both the logical and feeling parts of the issue during a dialogue. Your spouse will appreciate it. For example, Mike was unhappy at work and wanted to switch careers. He spoke of his frustrations but didn't speak of any organized plan he had to find another job. Believing he was too emotional, Marcia reminded him of their mortgage payments. He felt she was insensitive. She felt she was being realistic. Things improved when Mike also spoke of the practical side to job hunting, and when Marcia acknowledged how hard it must be to work at an unfulfilling job.

Plan ahead of time how to approach any hot topic. If you know, for example, that the upcoming discussion on whether to have a baby won't be easy, discuss your expectations with your spouse. Decide early that you'd like the discussion to be balanced (logic and emotion) and determine how that might best be achieved.

Keep in Mind

- If you could successfully transform your spouse into someone just like you, you really wouldn't enjoy the "new him."

- Opposites "attract" and opposites "detract." Emphasizing your partner's strengths and assets promotes satisfaction and teamwork.

Secret #8

Not Always Compromising

Rich wanted to go to the movies with Diane. All day he imagined his arm around her, the smell of popcorn, maybe a drink afterward. Then he remembered. Tonight was her karate class. Frustrated, he thought of renting a videotape instead. It wouldn't be as much fun, but they could watch it when she returned from her class, he decided.

So when Diane came home after her class and nonchalantly said she was too tired to watch the movie, Rich got mad. And she couldn't understand what all the hubbub was about.

The Problem With Compromising

One of the old standbys in marital relationships is compromising. Compromising couples are supposedly mature, unselfish, and considerate. And a marriage high on compromise is a marriage low in conflict. Right? Not necessarily. Rich compromised by buying a videotape instead of asking Diane to skip her karate class. Did it help? No. He resented it when she was too tired to watch it with him. That is one difficulty with compromises: it often makes you feel owed, and you resent it if you don't get your due.

Psychologist Daniel Wile believes that compromises are calculated risks.[1] Couples gamble that they can do something they really don't want to do without resenting it. Too often, what appears to be a stubborn, *uncompromising* mate, is really a frustrated partner who has compromised too much in the past—often unwittingly. How many times have you settled for something—a trip to your in-laws, a different television program, pizza instead of chow mein—but never bothered to inform your partner of your kindness in compromising? Couples do that frequently. It's nice, and it's one part of the give-and-take of marriage. But if you've made too many "hidden" compromises, and now feel a bit resentful or unappreciated, you may flatly refuse to budge on some new issue. What now appears to be stubbornness and selfishness grew out of your flexibility and selflessness.

One researcher studied the same couples over three years. The marriages that were happiest *in the short run* had wives who compromised a great deal. But over three years, those same marriages sharply *deteriorated* in satisfaction.[2] Taking an uncompromising stand once in a while helped inoculate marriages against future distress.

When should you not compromise? Generally speaking, don't compromise your values or your health. Don't compromise if you know you'll resent it later or if you'll feel owed. If it's a great sacrifice to compromise, well, that is sometimes necessary. But it's best to do so with the attitude that your sacrifice is a gift for the relationship. You may lose out in the short run, but only in the short run.

How can you be sure you aren't compromising too much or too little?

What to Do

Cut back on "hidden compromises." The more open you are about some of your thoughtful compromises, the more likely your spouse will be to show appreciation (and the less likely you'll be resentful). Understand that hidden compromises often involve *mind reading*—believing you know what your mate is thinking and feeling without asking. Reduce mind reading and you automatically reduce the number of hidden compromises. So the next time you talk yourself out of going to the opera because you "know" your mate won't want to go, try telling her, "I wasn't going to ask you to attend the opera with me because you don't usually like the opera. But I thought I'd ask you anyway. Would you like to go this time?"

If you won't compromise on an issue, be sure to show compassion. Saying, "I know it's a real sacrifice for you, but it's very important to do it my way this time" shows understanding and sensitivity for your mate. When your partner agrees to do things your way, say "Thank you" and mean it.

Give yourself and your mate a separate "special day" free from having to compromise. Remember when you were little and you were treated special on your birthday? Well, once every four to six weeks, give your partner a special day. Anything he wants, he gets. *Anything?* Well, within reasonable bounds. It's not recommended to spend an exorbitant amount of money or have one's way over a hot, divisive issue. The goal is to have fun and indulge in some extra selfish pleasure. Get the idea?

If you know you'll resent it if you compromise, it's best to talk about that *rather than to maintain an uncompromising stance.* Resentment is a sign of unsettled hurt. If you can discuss and settle the old issue, you may discover it's now easy to compromise on the current issue.

Keep in Mind

- Taking a firm, uncompromising stand now and then can actually make your mate feel good. Spouses appreciate an opportunity to make sacrifices for one another.

- Think twice before compromising your values or your health.

- If you resist being uncompromising because you don't wish to be "selfish," you'll eventually feel needy and expect your partner to meet those needs for you.

- The benefits of compromising evaporate if you resent it later. Better to discuss your potential resentment beforehand.

- A non-compromising stand may be a cover for old, unsettled hurts (such as feeling unappreciated or placed in a one-down position to your mate). Always compromising may mask your fear of rocking the boat.

Secret #9

Not Withdrawing from Conflict or Conversation

"I can't cope with it when she raises her voice," said one husband about his wife.

"If things get too hot, I'll just clam up. Why fan the fires by continuing to talk?" another husband stated.

"If it makes no difference what I say, why bother?"

These statements are typical for many people, especially men. The emerging truth seems to be that men who might otherwise thrive in a Marine boot-camp, thrill to cut-throat competition, scoff at the pain from a serious sports injury, or drive a car in New York City traffic can't handle conflict—or even benign but lengthy conversations—with their wives.

It's not hard to understand why many people prefer to withdraw from the scene when conflict arises. Conflicts heighten anxiety, often get worse before they get better, and stir up resentments thought long passed. Conflicts slash the hope that the relationship might be better than most. And they frequently ruin an evening, alarm the children, and frighten the dog. Arguments are serious business. But conflict-avoidance is risky business. Particularly when motivated by fear ("It will only make him madder") or a futile, defeated sense of "why bother," people who avoid conflict *actually increase their chances of fighting in the future.* Resentments and frustrations don't stay idle in the minds and hearts of dissatisfied partners. And when a conflict finally erupts and is not handled successfully, *it increases the odds the partners will actively avoid more arguments in the future.* Essentially, a vicious cycle develops: conflict-avoidance frustrates a spouse, which leads to an increase in (often unproductive) arguments, resulting in more conflict-avoidance.

Snared on a merry-go-round of unsatisfying interactions, no wonder some couples feel blue.

How to Hang in There

Julie wasn't having any success getting her point across.

"Steve," she said, "if you want to have a quick beer with Jerry after work some days I don't mind. But I need you to call me first."

"I don't understand why I always have to do that," Steve answered. "I arrive home only a half-hour later than usual and we don't have dinner until after seven, so what's the big deal? I feel like I have to get your permission."

"I'm not giving you permission . . ." she began, but Steve had heard it too many times before. So once again he tuned her out. He wasn't even looking at her now. He sat subdued; his body was present but his mind was elsewhere.

"See what I mean?" Julie said, turning to me, exasperated. "He shuts me out." Then, with a twinge of guilt, she added, "I don't like to nag, but he frustrates me so."

Men like Steve often shut down during arguments and sometimes during neutral conversations they fear might turn into an argument. Sometimes they leave the room instead. Or they shift the topic to something irrelevant but safer. But essentially they *withdraw*—and it might have its basis in biology.

Researcher John Gottman recruited married couples and hooked them up to monitors that measured physiological responses (such as heart rate and blood pressure) during disagreements.[1] The results? Men's physiological arousal jumped quickly to a level significantly higher than the women's, resulting in what researcher Ron Levant aptly dubbed "the buzz." To men, "the buzz" was a highly uncomfortable bodily experience characterized by such things as indistinct muscle tension, vague stomach distress, a constriction in the throat, rapid pulse, and a general antsiness. Experiencing the buzz, a man is preoccupied with the thought, "I gotta get out of here!"

In contrast, wives did not experience noticeable discomfort. For them, expressing anger eventually led to a reduction in their physiological arousal.

"Stonewalling" is one way men cope with the buzz. Gottman describes it as the avoidance of eye-contact, keeping one's face still, and not using common vocalizations like "Uh-huh" that would tell the speaker he is paying attention to her. A wife who screams, "I feel like I'm talking to a brick wall!" probably is.

When husbands stonewalled, marital happiness greatly diminished over time.

A husband's stonewalling was usually followed by his wife trying to re-engage his interest. If that didn't work, she became critical and disgusted. Eventually, after repeated failed attempts to draw her husband into conversations, she withdrew from him.

When both husband and wife stubbornly withdrew and felt defensive, the marriage was at very high risk for eventual separation or divorce.

Astonishingly, based on heart rate alone, researchers predicted with over 85 percent accuracy which relationships would improve and which would deteriorate over five years. Couples whose hearts beat faster, whose blood flowed faster, and who sweated more during an argument showed significant declines in marital satisfaction several years later. Conversely, *calmer couples had marriages that improved over time.* That finding is stronger than the research linking cholesterol level with heart disease!

In order to reduce withdrawal, ways to reduce anxiety and discomfort during conversation must be found.

What to Do

Remain seated while talking. You then reduce the risk of intimidating postures and premature exits. In any conversation, emotions are more likely to flare when you are in a standing position than when you are seated.

Breathe properly. Under stress we all tend to breathe more shallowly and rapidly—adding to our physical discomfort. Researcher James Lynch discovered that proper breathing during stressful conversations significantly lowered pulse rate and blood pressure.[2]

The simplest way to reduce anxiety is to breathe through your lower abdomen or diaphragm. You know you are breathing properly through your diaphragm when your stomach puffs out as you inhale. Diaphragmatic breathing lowers your level of anxiety almost immediately. Breathing like that while talking with a spouse can calm you and curb your inclination to withdraw emotionally from conversations.

Speak slowly and softly. A 1990 study reported what happened when participants were asked to discuss anger-arousing events using three different voice styles: fast and loud; slow and soft; and normal conversational tone. Men and women both had a much higher rise in blood pressure and heart rate, *and they felt much more anger,* when they spoke in the fast/loud style compared to their normal speaking voice. These same people had much lower pulse and blood pressure readings *and felt significantly less anger* when they spoke slowly and softly.[3]

When discussing hot topics, practicing speaking more softly and slower than usual will reduce your frustrations and improve the odds you won't withdraw from the conversation.

Call a time-out if the discussion gets too uncomfortable or unproductive. A time-out is not a withdrawal as long as there is an agreement to resume the discussion after a break. During the break you might go for a walk, take a shower, listen to music, make a phone call—something distracting, enjoyable, and calming. If it's very late, rescheduling the discussion until the next day is perfectly acceptable.

Keep in Mind

- The most common wish by even the most satisfied wives is that their husbands would talk more.

Did You Know...

... that distressed couples spend much more time in conflict than do happier couples? But according to researchers Patricia Noller and Mary Anne Fitzpatrick in the *Journal of Marriage and the Family*, distressed couples also *avoid* conflict much more frequently than nondistressed couples. In other words, less-than-satisfied couples deplete their amount of quality time together by both actively fighting and actively avoiding fights (via withdrawal or silence). In comparison, happy couples fight less often and spend the rest of their shared time enjoying each other's company.*

* Noller, Patricia & Fitzpatrick, Mary Anne. Marital communication in the eighties. *Journal of Marriage and the Family, 52,* 1990, 832-843.

- A man's withdrawal from marital discussions may not be a character flaw but a reaction to physical discomfort.

- Responding with appreciation to his willingness to "hang in there" during discussions is helpful. Saying, "Why give credit for something he should do anyway?" is not. Responding with appreciation to her willingness to go at a pace more comfortable for you is helpful. Taking her cooperativeness for granted is not.

Secret #10

Enjoying Time Together

Imagine having a neighbor you don't get along with very well. Oh, he's friendly and all, but pretend he's the kind of neighbor who borrows tools and forgets to return them. Or he tells ethnic jokes (about *your* ethnic heritage). Or he uses your lawn mower one Saturday because his broke down, and six Saturdays later he's still using your mower—and your gasoline.

Imagine that the two of you have little in common (this is a stretch, I know). He trivializes sports and you're an expert in sports trivia. He's an electronics whiz and you still can't program your VCR. Do you know what you two could do to turn your relationship around? How about a weekend trip together! After forty-eight hours of lei-surely, fun time, you'll be best buddies.

It doesn't work that way in marriages, either.

Happiest couples do spend more leisure time together. In one re-cent study of 250 people (married an average of twelve years), the best predictor of marital satisfaction was the amount of leisure time spent alone with one's spouse. In particular, wives who spent the least time with their husbands were the most unhappy.[1] But does spending time together improve marital satisfaction, or do happier couples simply spend more time together?

Researcher Lynn White interviewed two thousand couples to de-termine how spending time together promoted happiness.[2] Her hy-pothesis was that couples with dual careers, children, and hobbies would spend less time together and consequently be less happy. That wasn't always true. What mostly determined whether couples spent time together was the quality of their marriage. The happier they were, the more time they shared, despite obvious constraints (kids, jobs, etc.). So throwing a couple in a hotel room for a weekend and saying "Have fun!" isn't a good idea if the partners are already dissatisfied. For some couples, too much too soon is too risky.

"Morning" vs. "Night" Partners

Most satisfied partners will tell you that their time alone together is special, that it keeps their friendship alive. But leisure time is at a premium these days. And it's complicated by this fact: one-quarter of all two-income couples do "shift" work. So when the husband works evenings and the wife works days, how do they spend time alone together? And when partners don't work separate shifts, some are mismatched by being a "morning" or a "night" person (a "lark" or an "owl"). ("Larks" love sunrises, breakfast, and the great outdoors and generally feel more energetic the first part of the day. "Owls" savor sleeping late and the night-life and "can't get moving" until the middle of the afternoon.)

A 1991 study showed that mismatched (night vs. morning) couples spent less time in shared activities each week (three hours, as opposed to six hours for "matched" couples). And their overall level of satisfaction was lower than that of their counterparts.[3] However, with the right adjustments, owls and larks learned to improve their satisfaction levels.

In order to enjoy more time together, two factors must be present: the *desire* to spend time, and the *opportunity*. The happiest couples have the desire and make the opportunity.

What to Do

To improve opportunity, schedule shared activities. Go to your wall calendar and set a date. Knowing ahead of time, for example, that after dinner on Thursday the two of you will go for a stroll improves the odds you won't get sidetracked by phone calls, mail sorting, or dirty dishes. Keeping to your schedule means saying "No" to low-priority outside events. (Note: you may feel awkward "scheduling" your partner. But after the first few times you'll be surprised at how natural—and workable—the strategy is.)

To improve opportunity, make the "mundane" special. Every couple must (sooner or later) discuss current events (bills, the children, local gossip, home repairs, etc.) Discuss those topics while taking some pleasurable time together, such as a ten-minute walk. Discuss a phone conversation you had while giving your mate a back rub, or while cuddling in bed, or while scrubbing his back. Watching TV together? Make popcorn, put your arm around your mate, and pretend you're at the movie theater. Discussing what's for dinner? Pop in your favorite cassette and do a slow dance. Confer about world events while brushing your wife's hair (she'll love it). Chat while massaging your husband's feet. Do you like to exercise? Try exercising together once in a while.

Brainstorm about fun and different activities you'd like to do (this is a great exercise to do while passing the time on a long drive together). Make each activity begin with each letter of the alphabet (go Antiquing, Bake bread, rent a Canoe, take a Dance class, Eat lunch outdoors, Fly a kite, etc.). Or, come up with as many activities as possible beginning with a certain letter (go Skating, go Skinny dipping, Sunbathe, create an exotic Sundae, Skip rope, Sing to your children, purchase a colorful pair of Shorts, etc.).

Add to your list any activities you might enjoy if you were on vacation. You don't need to actually be on vacation to enjoy sightseeing, backpacking, renting a boat, eating out two nights in a row, playing badminton, playing Monopoly, making love in the middle of the afternoon, etc.

Spouses who claim they have no common interests have simply let their creativity go stale. As you can see, there are dozens of enjoyable activities you and your mate could consider. It's as easy as A-B-C.

Take turns making it one person's "day" to dictate what special, pleasant activity you can do together. Agree ahead of time that you can't say "No" to the request. Activities should take no longer than thirty minutes (although you can spend more time if both agree). Use the list you created in previous exercises or come up with new ideas. This exercise improves the odds that sharing activities won't be forgotten. And it insures that the same spouse isn't always the one "in charge" of the couple's time together.

Visualize. To improve your desire, think of a place you would spend a lovely weekend at. Now, think of three people (including your spouse) that you regularly spend time with. Consider going to that place with each —one at a time.[4] Visualize each scenario as fully as possible. Now consider going alone. Finally, consider going with someone other than the above. Now, which was the least and most satisfying experience? How did your spouse fare? If your spouse was the most enjoyable person to be with, lucky you. If not, what qualities of the person you most enjoyed might you be able to encourage in your spouse?

Make minor adjustments to your sleep-wake pattern if one of you is a "night person" and the other is a "morning person."[5] Staying out a little later than you'd like or rising earlier than you'd prefer is not too much to ask once in a while. A "night" wife shouldn't call her husband "boring" because he likes to be asleep by 10 pm. A "morning" husband shouldn't call his wife "lazy" because she could sleep until noon. If you have an infant, the "night" parent can care for the fussy baby at 1:00am while the "morning" parent can care for a fussy child at 5:30am. If your children are older, the "morning" spouse can see the kids off to school, the "night" spouse can stay up late waiting for your teenager to arrive home from a date. Show appreciation for *any* changes your spouse makes in her sleep-wake schedule to accommodate you.

Did You Know . . .

. . . the 1980s saw a tremendous decline in the total number of leisure hours available to the average household. A 1991 report on couples with two children showed that from 1978 to 1988, the average woman increased her time on the job by eleven hours per week—most at the expense of her leisure time. Hours doing household chores declined for women by 3.5 hours per week, but their husbands picked up the slack by adding 3.5 hours to their weekly chore duty—also at the expense of their leisure time. The upshot? Working couples are busier than ever, and the first thing to go by the wayside was shared couple activities.*

* Zick, C.B. & McCullough, J.L. Trends in married couples' time use: evidence from 1977-78 and 1987-88. *Sex Roles*, 1991, 24(7-8), 459-487.

Keep in Mind

- If you wait until you have several hours of leisure time together, you'll miss out on dozens of opportunities to enjoy your partner's company. Think small.

- If you don't have time for leisure because you have too much to do, you have too much to do.[6]

- You and your mate don't have to have similar interests to enjoy time with one another.

- Happy partners are good friends. Friends need time alone together.

Effective Problem Solving

On a television talk show, the newlywed couple being interviewed discuss their marital concerns. She thinks he's spending too much time watching television and too little time in conversation with her. He claims he watches only a few favorite programs.

"Oh no," she retorts, "you turn that television on *every* night."

"If I do, it's only because you're on the phone with your mother and I'm bored. I think you haven't quite 'cut the cord' with her, by the way."

"I don't understand how you can say that . . ."

And off they go.

The cameras pan for the audience reaction and what do you see? Slight grins, some chuckling, nods of the head. Some audience members smile at the memory of having had a similar problem, a problem they now regard as minor, common in young marriages, and settled. Ever look back on an argument you had years ago with your mate and wonder how the two of you got so upset over what you'd now regard as hardly a problem at all? ("What do you mean you don't like my haircut?") In hindsight, you often see how you overreacted to some difficulty. But at the time you're experiencing a problem, it's hard to believe you are making mountains out of molehills.

The Problem with Problem-Solving

Solving the common problems that arise in a marriage is like assembling a child's plastic tricycle: it's so simple, but nine out of ten times you'll mess it up. Typically, three factors can make problem-solving a problem in your marriage.

- Some couples believe that if a problems crops up in their relationship, they've got a PROBLEM. Something must be wrong, they conclude, if we run into difficulties. Intellectually, spouses know problems will occasionally arise. But they are often shocked and dismayed when it happens. The realization that an argument doesn't mean divorce eventually puts those couples at ease.

- When problem-solving efforts falter, or when certain problems repeatedly arise, the couple now has two problems: the original difficulty and the bad feelings that have erupted (resentment, depression, guilt, or worry) as a consequence of the first problem. If you and your mate can't agree on discipline for the kids (the original problem), you may regard him as bull-headed and inconsiderate. *That* attitude is now a problem and will likely interfere the next time you and your mate discuss discipline.

  John and Kathy had longstanding marital problems. In an effort to improve the emotional atmosphere, they made reservations for a romantic dinner at a restaurant. Their date was pleasant but punctuated by many awkward and uncomfortable moments. Each was afraid to say or do "the wrong thing." The next day, each was more pessimistic about their marriage. "We couldn't relax and enjoy each other's company," they explained grimly.

  "But that was to be expected," I said. "Your problem was not that you were uncomfortable with each other but that *you were uncomfortable about being uncomfortable.*" Had they been able to shrug off their discomfort as being normal, they might have relaxed.

- Effective problem-solving is a skill. It takes practice, and certain guidelines should be followed. Presuming you or your mate should already possess adequate problem-solving skills is a mistake. By definition, a problem is something you can't handle right away. If you could, it wouldn't be a problem.

Four Steps To Effective Problem-Solving
1. *Identify the problem.* If you have several related problems,

choose one for discussion. Be specific. Stating, "We don't see eye to eye on discipline" is too vague. Saying "When I discipline the kids and you disagree with my approach, you debate me in front of the children," is clear and precise. Problem identification is easier when you can separate facts (observable behavior) from assumptions (internal beliefs). "You just told the Hendersons we'd attend their barbecue on Sunday without consulting me" is a fact. "You don't consider my feelings" is an assumption. (Partners are much more willing to admit to observable behaviors ("You're right. I did tell the Hendersons we'd see them on Sunday.") than agree to assumptions ("You're wrong. I *do* consider your feelings.").

2. *Brainstorm possible solutions.* List as many potential solutions as you can, no matter how off-beat they appear. (Couples frequently lock themselves into believing that only one or two legitimate solutions exist.) As you do so, rate from 0 to 100 percent how well that solution meets your needs.[1] For example, one solution to a disagreement over discipline was: my husband should not contradict me when I'm dealing with the children. The wife believed that solution met 100 percent of her needs, but the husband said it met only 10 percent of his needs. He wanted the opportunity to discuss his views when he disagreed with her. A new proposed solution was that, when possible, they'd discuss what to do before intervening with the children, but that if they couldn't agree on a strategy, the wife could do what she wanted 50 percent of the time.

3. *Select one proposed solution.* Solutions that maximize the needs for each is the best one to try. Be sure to discuss *when* the solution will first be attempted (and how frequently), *who* will initiate it, and *how long* you will try it.

4. *Evaluate your progress.* Don't think only in terms of success or failure. Often the tried solution to a problem needs fine tuning. Did the solution make a positive difference? Is it worth continuing or modifying? What made the solution easier to enact? What impeded your performance? Remember the "Thirty Day Rule" from chapter 1. Making an honest effort

for thirty days prevents you from abandoning efforts at the first hint of difficulty.

Despite guidelines to effective problem-solving, couples commonly get bogged down in their efforts. The following strategies can help you eliminate "problem-solving" from your list of problems to be solved.

What to Do

Rehearse the four steps to effective problem solving by discussing an issue that is *not* a problem for you. Do you and your mate agree on financial matters? Do you have wonderful relationships with your in-laws? Good. Pretend you don't and review the steps to problem-solving. Problem-solving is like CPR (cardio-pulmonary resuscitation): you don't wait until you have a crisis to learn how to do it.

If a problem is recurrent, you'll have to manage any emotional side-effects first (resentment, hopelessness, outbursts, unfair accusations, etc.) before you contend with the problem itself. Most people believe that bad feelings are a secondary consequence and will diminish as soon as a problem is resolved. But when a problem becomes chronic, the reverse is true: until you can soothe the negative feelings, you may never solve your problem.

Bill and Cindy argued constantly about money. He felt she was too careless in her spending, she believed he was too rigid and controlling. Working on a budget was useless because neither one believed the other showed caring or understanding. Until that was corrected, progress on the budget was slow. Soothing hurt feelings is best accomplished by reflective listening (see chapter 2).

Consider these three commonly overlooked features to effective problem-solving:

- Evaluate your role in the problem before you evaluate your partner's role. It reduces blaming and improves cooperation.

- List all previously attempted solutions. Some should clearly not be attempted again, but others may still have merit. If a solution failed before, did you give it an honest try? If a solution "worked" but the same problem eventually reappeared, perhaps the answer is to try it again but for a longer period.

● Keep in mind areas of agreement. You may disagree about discipline, for example, but remember that you each want what's best for your children.

Select a problem you successfully solved together and ask one another, *"What happened that allowed us to solve that problem successfully?"* Pinpointing factors that contributed to your success ("We were patient" or "There was no yelling") can help you determine how to improve the current situation.[2]

Go somewhere else to resolve your problems. (More arguments occur in the kitchen than in any other room in the house.) If the house is noisy or the kitchen table is cluttered, sit outside at a picnic table. Or agree to have a "business lunch" with your mate at a restaurant. Do it again the next day if you have more to discuss. Talk while one (or both) of you is relaxing in a hot tub or bubble bath. Grab a Thermos of coffee and drive to a nearby park or some other scenic place. You can talk in your car or outdoors.

Often, doing *anything* different from your typical pattern of inter-action can be enough to put the two of you on a constructive track. The easiest thing to change is your location.

Watch your language. Avoid "catastrophic" phrases like "You're being

---

Did You Know . . .

. . . that problem-solving efforts marked by brief, hostile exchanges followed by withdrawal may indicate depression in one or both spouses?[4] People in discordant marriages are twenty-five times more likely to be depressed than partners in a satisfying relationship. (A woman dissatisfied with her marriage has a 50 percent chance of being clinically de-pressed.) Verbal confrontation and subsequent withdrawal impede problem-solving, which then adds to the depression.

On the plus side, when self-disclosure is encouraged and done in a structured manner (such as in the presence of a therapist), discussions can be beneficial and positive and may help to reduce depressive symptoms.

* Beach, S.R., Sandeen, E.E., & O'Leary, K.D. *Depression In Marriage.* New York: Guilford, 1990, p. 17, 79-80.

impossible" or "This is totally unworkable." Most problems couples face are workable. They might also be *inconvenient, discomforting, irritating,* but not impossible. Avoid talking in "absolutes" such as "We *must* solve this" or "You *should* agree with me." (Better to say, "I'd *like it if . . .*").

If nothing else works, agree to be arbitrary. Psychologist Michelle Weiner-Davis recommends sometimes tossing a coin.[3] If it's heads, handle the problem your way. If it's tails, handle it your partner's way. Knowing ahead of time that the decision will be made by a coin flip if the two of you can't agree may motivate each of you to resolve the problem sooner.

Keep in Mind

- Happy couples have their problems. But they also possess faith in their ability to cope with problems.

- Regarding your problem as a challenge instead of as a threat may help you work together as a cooperative team.

- If problem-solving efforts fail, you may choose to avoid such efforts in the future. But avoidance or withdrawal reduces intimacy and confidence and ultimately adds more problems to your list.

- You are models for your children. How you handle strong differences of opinion and impasses with your mate is just as educational as how well you cooperate.

- The resolution to some problems may require great sacrifice on your spouse's part. Gratitude and caring is important.

Secret #12

Being a Cheerleader for Your Mate

The graduation ceremony finally ended. Hordes of twenty-two year olds in caps and gowns hooted and hollered, while the family and friends from the bleacher seats cascaded into the throng. And somewhere in the mass of people, Lisa, thirty-eight and mother of three, held her cap tightly to her head while she searched for her husband Art.

"Congratulations, graduate!" said a familiar voice. Lisa turned around to see Art, all smiles and holding a single yellow rose. She hugged him tightly, grateful for the husband who encouraged her every step of the way, even when he had to take a back seat to her studies.

Your mate probably has personal dreams of glory or accomplishment—some realistic, some pie-in-the-sky. Maybe she'd like to start her own business or learn to fly an airplane, maybe he'd like to buy a parcel of land and build, with his own hands, your vacation cottage. Maybe you'd like to join the community theater or run for a local office. Or run in a marathon. Or do regular volunteer work for a charity organization. Or write a children's book. Or learn to ride a horse. Or create a country garden second to none.

Dreams don't have to be fanciful to be meaningful. Joe's fantasy was to buy a canoe and take his wife to the nearby lake every weekend. Carol wanted to practice something she hadn't done in thirty years—ice skating. "Wouldn't it be great if . . ." If what? What's your dream?

"Oh, Ralph. Not again!"

Remember "The Honeymooners"? Ralph Kramden would concoct some get-rich-quick scheme, only to have it fail. His wife, Alice, had no faith in Ralph's ideas and repeatedly told him so. He'd be angry with her in a manner that, to the audience, was funny and entertaining.

But it wasn't funny to Ralph. He wanted support and encouragement. What he got was criticism.

Some spouses discourage a mate's ideas because they view them as impractical. ("We can't afford it. And what do you know about chicken farming, anyway?") But such comments often have the reverse effect. Challenging your mate often prompts him to come up with reasons why the idea *can* work. More importantly, if your spouse regards you as unsupportive, he'll distance himself from you emotionally and probably spend more time fantasizing about his dream.

Discouragement is often a clue that the idea is scary, not necessarily impractical. Your partner might be scared because your dreams clash with his expectations of your life together. (Secretly, spouses sometimes feel threatened by a mate's fanciful wishes.) Her dream or challenging goal suggests to you that your mate *needs more from her life than she's currently getting*—something you translate as "I'm not good enough for her."

People fantasize more than they act on their fantasies. Most of the time your spouse just wants to dream aloud, not engage in a serious discussion of the idea. Encouraging your partner's ideas, or simply agreeing, "Yeah, that sounds exciting," does no harm and builds closeness. Whether or not dreams get acted upon is less important than how close you feel to one another at the time.

One troublesome phenomenon occurs when one spouse believes the other is "holding me back." Hank wanted to start his own auto mechanic business. In truth, he had many misgivings about the idea ("What if I go bankrupt?") and wasn't sure he'd attempt it even if given the opportunity. But when his wife Jane pointed out some concerns of her own, he got angry. He abandoned his dream but blamed Jane for it. If she could only be supportive, he thought, his dream would come true. Actually, Jane wasn't holding Hank back. Hank was. He was afraid to try for fear he'd fail. But rather than admit that, he conveniently blamed Jane.

That's another good reason to be supportive of your mate's dreams: if they don't materialize, you won't be blamed.

Remember when you were dating? Each of you probably spoke of many dreams you had for the future. One main reason you kept on dating was that your partner didn't discourage your dreams. He listened intently and enthusiastically. You felt free to relax and be yourself with him. Just because you're married doesn't mean you stop dreaming. And *because* you are married is one good reason to care about your spouse's goals and dreams. That's what friends are for.

What to Do

Play a game of "Wouldn't it be great if . . ." the next time you have an opportunity to chat. Initiate the discussion so your mate knows you're interested in her fantasies. Be as encouraging as possible. Even if you don't like your spouse's ideas, get her to elaborate by asking "And then what would you do?"

If you must express a discouraging word, do so only after your partner has expressed his ideas as fully as possible. Use the reflective listening technique (see page 23) so your mate will believe you've listened and understood before you give your view. Don't immediately point out the faults of your mate's dream—that appears critical and unfeeling. Instead, talk about how the idea *worries* or *scares* or *concerns* you. Saying "It worries me that you'll have less time with the family if you start this project" doesn't imply the project is a bad idea.

Applaud your mate's accomplishments, even if you wish he were doing something else. If his role in the community play takes time from his being able to mow the lawn, mow it for him (or hire someone) with no complaints. Is your wife taking a college course, and for the past three months has spent more time studying than talking to you? Help type her term paper and congratulate her on her B+.

If your spouse is already involved in some project and there is no turning back, periodic complaints and verbal jabs are poisonous. If you are feeling frustrated or overwhelmed by your partner's project, report those feelings without acting on them. Saying, "I know you have to rehearse your lines for the play today, but this is one of those times I'm feeling overwhelmed" may bring you the support you desire. Complaining, "Why won't you do what I want for a change?" won't.

If you resent your partner's dream-building activities, you feel owed. Think what it is your partner owes you. A simple "Thanks"? A day off occasionally where the two of you together—or you alone—can enjoy some free time? A willingness to support you in *your* dream? Resentment can eat away at the foundation of your relationship. Clear the air, but don't be accusatory and hostile. Say, "I thought I could deal with this project of yours, but I'm finding it more difficult than I expected. I have some ideas on what could help."

Keep in Mind

- It's easy to be excited for your mate when her project excites you, too. Most often, however, you need to be excited *because your mate is excited*, even if the idea doesn't thrill you.

- Reflexively pointing out the flaws in your mate's dream can reflect a parental "I know better" attitude. Your mate wants a partner, not a parent.

- A supportive spouse is not necessarily one who agrees fully with your goals. In fact, a spouse who doesn't step in your way despite misgivings may be the most supportive of all.

- One thing is for sure: whether you support or impede your spouse in her dreams, she'll never forget.

Secret #13

Halting Arguments the Right Way

"I thought this was supposed to be *our* weekend away together, Bill. I can't believe you invited Dick and Sheila."

"I thought you'd enjoy having Sheila around. Besides, we'll have plenty of time to be alone," Bill answered crossly. "Sometimes I can't figure you out at all, Liz. You've wanted the four of us to go skiing for a long time. That's all I heard you talk about last summer."

"But what I meant was . . ."

"You always mean something other than you say," Bill interrupted. "Why is it you can't hear your own words the way everyone else hears them? I really wish you'd . . . ."

Here we go again, Liz thought to herself, tuning Bill out. It's not worth arguing about, she concluded. Sullen, she resigned herself to end the argument and go skiing with Bill, Dick, and Sheila. What a romantic weekend that would be.

And the argument did end, at least the *verbal* argument ended. But the non-verbal argument was just beginning. Over the next several days Bill could tell something was wrong. Liz was standoffish, irritable, and too quiet. Here we go again, Bill thought to himself.

It Ain't Over 'Til It's Over

One of the most outstanding features of unhappy couples is their inability to end negative, hurtful interactions.[1] Their arguments fit this pattern:

1. The argument escalates as each partner gets more and more angry and hostile.

2. Escalations are punctuated by periodic attempts by either

partner to calm the situation. When the effort to de-escalate the argument has no immediate impact, that partner resumes hostilities.

3. The argument "ends" by one partner shutting down or withdrawing from the scene (as Liz did with Bill). But the argument continues on a non-verbal level.

What has been popularly referred to as a "power struggle" occurs when battling partners believe they've been treated unjustly by their mate. Trying to balance the scales of justice by coercive means (making demands, punishing, hinting, withdrawing) often comes next but is rarely satisfying. "Look what I have to go through to get you to do things my way" is a common complaint of unhappy, coercive couples.

Another complication with coercion has to do with a principle in social psychology: if someone acts a certain way despite very strong constraints (for example, if a jogger is running outside in sub-zero weather), we conclude there is great motivation to do so. So if a husband observes his wife repeatedly complaining to him despite his efforts to stop her (by withdrawing and "refusing to listen"), he concludes that his wife must have a strong motivation to keep complaining. (She's stubborn and doesn't want to consider my feelings, he'll probably conclude.) But the same principle applies to the wife. She observes her husband to be withdrawn and uncommunicative despite her strong protests. So she concludes he must be highly motivated to act that way. (He's being stubborn and doesn't want to consider my feelings, she'll probably conclude.) When coercive efforts fail to bring about the desired response, couples often decide to act *more* coercively. Rarely do they see how the coercive efforts make their partners more hurt and angry and therefore contribute to the problem.

Arguments must end sometime, but how they end is more important than when. Do your "buttons get pushed" during arguments with your spouse? If so, pushing back will fuel the fires, not douse them. The first step in halting hurtful escalations is acknowledging that they are problematic and need changing.

What to Do

Split the week. You take Monday, Wednesday, and Friday. Your spouse takes Tuesday, Thursday, and Saturday. When it's your day, it is your responsibility to maintain a non-critical, non-punishing stance whatever your partner's actions. You refuse to accuse or coerce. Instead, state that you'll discuss the issue at hand only in a calm manner, preferably using the communication techniques suggested in chapter 2. This insures that one of you will keep a cool head while allowing the other to vent, if necessary.

Call attention to the fact that your "button has been pushed" without inflaming the situation. A clever and creative way to do that is the following: each of you pockets seven pennies.[2] Every time you believe your spouse pushes your buttons, you give him or her a penny. (A fundamental rule of this game is that the penny-giver is always right. There is no debate.) The goal is to have as few of your mate's pennies in your possession as possible. This exercise interrupts your automatic exchanges before they get too intense.

Schedule a discussion (argument?) but record it on audio- or videotape. (Don't dismiss this idea too readily. Couples who try this more effectively alter their behavior.) Listen to the tape alone and then together. Then try to list three "unproductive" things you said or did. Discuss them with your partner. Don't debate whether either of you had a "right" to say what you said. The purpose of the exercise is to help you recognize your unhelpful contributions to marital arguments.

After you've made progress with these exercises, role-play a recent (constructive) discussion, but this time purposely *turn it into an argument by playing your former role.* Say and do the kinds of things you now know will only make matters worse (ideally, record it on video or audio). Afterward, discuss your reactions with each other. This exercise can have very subtle and powerful effects. Forcing yourself to be harsh and uncaring—in a contrived manner—makes you more acutely aware of the hurtful behaviors that once were so automatic and reflexive.

This is important: when the role-play is over, actually tell one another that you are not the person who was arguing a moment ago. Remind one another it was a role-play. Embrace, and do something enjoyable.

Touch base. When an argument ends (or is interrupted by the children, a phone call, work schedules, etc.) make some positive, tender, *physical* connection with your mate. It needn't be warm and loving (since you don't feel all that loving after an argument). Touch or squeeze your mate's hand, stroke his shoulder, give her a goodbye peck-on-the-cheek—do anything physical that indicates you're still connected to each other and that you want hurt feelings to somehow be mended. It is an immediate and powerful signal that you still care. (Deep down your mate knows you care, but at the moment he or she may feel unsure.)

Keep in Mind

- Withdrawing from an argument is a short-term solution with long-term negative consequences. Hang in there.

- Don't develop the attitude that you will show kindness and consideration during a discussion *only if* your mate is showing it. Research shows that happier couples are more tolerant, understanding, and empathic even when their mates are not.

- Appreciate any and all efforts by your mate to argue more effectively. He or she needs your support.

Secret #14

A Special Way of Caring

Here's the scenario: Jim comes home late from work. He greets his wife warmly; she responds a bit stiffly. "I knew you were going to be too busy today, so I picked up your dry-cleaning for you," he says. "And here is a bottle of wine. I was hoping we could enjoy a glass together after the kids go to sleep." Janet gives a slight nod in Jim's direction, hardly acknowledging him, mumbles "Thanks" and without even a smile directs her attention back to the rambunctious children. Not saying another word, Jim puts the wine in the refrigerator.

Knowing nothing else about this couple, would you guess there was some underlying conflict or problem in this relationship? If so, you've probably bought into the myth that happy couples are quick to show gratitude and appreciation.

Actually, Jim and Janet have a happy marriage. Fact: happy couples who have young children are less likely to react immediately and positively to a partner's kindness, according to the studies conducted by highly respected researcher and family therapist Neil Jacobson.[1] The positive reaction may never even come, but some caring or considerate action eventually will. The partners know that and therefore don't feel neglected or unappreciated. They can tolerate the wait. Unhappy couples are different. Their satisfaction in the marriage is closely tied to the "What have you done for me lately?" attitude. They are much more likely than happy couples to have a strong, *immediate* emotional reaction (positive or negative) to their partner's actions. Learning to give to one's spouse without automatically expecting appreciation is a task for couples wanting to be more satisfied in their marriage. But that only happens when, deep down, a spouse knows her partner cares.

Caring About Caring

Even couples in love wake up some mornings not feeling in love. The emotion of love often comes in waves. Some days you know it's "out there" but it hasn't yet rolled in to greet you. And that's okay. But that normal response is frightening to couples having marital problems. They wonder if not feeling in love means they've fallen *out* of love.

When the feeling of love has receded, it's important to focus on caring. You can care without loving, but there is no love without caring. The knowledge—the experience—of being cared about by a partner often deepens commitment, inspires intimacy, and sparks passion.

When a couple successfully ends marriage therapy, I often ask them "What worked? What made the biggest difference in resolving your differences?" Roberta's answer was typical. "Finally believing that Steve understood—no, more than that—believing he *cared* about my feelings even if he disagreed with me. That's what made it work for me."

Happier couples care about caring.

Caring: Money in the Relationship Bank

When your bank account is nearly empty, every deposit or withdrawal is keenly felt. In relationships, every act of love or caring is like money in the relationship bank. Each argument or instance of uncaring is like a withdrawal from the account. To be happy, couples must have a reserve of love and caring to help through the rainy days in their relationship.[2]

How much caring is enough? Researcher John Gottman believes that a marriage can withstand conflict if the ratio of caring to conflict is ten to one.[3] The difficulty for severely distressed couples, however, is that an upsurge in caring doesn't *automatically* erase months or years of anger or unkindness. Commonly, one major argument for a dissatisfied couple can erase the effects of ten to twenty positive interactions. (Realizing that setbacks are part and parcel of changing can help those couples cope better; see chapter 1.) Fortunately, for the average, satisfied couple who wish to boost their overall happiness, "daily gestures of gratuitous kindness" are good medicine.[4]

Most partners believe they care. And they'll point to numerous acts they perform every day to prove it. But a funny thing happens on the way to your fifth wedding anniversary: actions once viewed as considerate and special by an appreciative spouse (filling the gas tank, sewing on a button) are now expected, and sometimes demanded. (In other words, you don't get credit for doing them anymore.) So when the wife exits an important meeting at work to pick up a sick child from school, her husband takes that for granted. And if the husband spends his Saturday installing a shelf-unit, his wife's attitude is "That's his job. He knows I have no talent for that and God knows we can't afford to hire someone else to do it." Where is the appreciation? (It evaporated about the same time watching a ball game or "getting a good night's sleep" was more fun than having sex.)

Knowing you are cared for and appreciated can keep your relationship boat from tipping over.

What to Do

Pinpoint ten to fifteen deeds you already do *that you know have a positive impact on your mate.*[5] Then do them more often. Your list might include making a meal for your mate, fixing her a cup of tea without being asked, showing appreciation or affection, vacuuming the interior of her car, meeting him for lunch, having coffee together before you go to work, tidying up, etc. This task helps you focus on *your* behavior—already in your repertoire.

Begin "caring days."[6] Each of you should draw up a list of at least ten small, non-conflictual things a partner could do that would make you feel cared for. Such things as, kiss me and hold me when you first arrive home; call me during the day to say "I love you"; massage my feet; send me a love note; enjoy a glass of wine with me; brush my hair; allow me fifteen minutes of free time when I first get home from work; clean the car; etc. The goal is to do three things a day from your partner's list. That is ninety *extra* caring tasks a month. Important: the tasks should be small, inexpensive, and require little time. They should be very specific. "Talk more to me" is vague. "Take ten minutes tonight and discuss how our day went" is specific. Most important of all, express thanks every time your partner shows caring. Appreciative comments encourage your mate. Silence may be interpreted as lack of interest or gratitude.

Extend caring to your partner even (especially) on days when he or she is neglecting you. During the end of the second week of Caring Days, each of you should secretly select one day out of the next seven where you will purposely reduce your demonstration of caring. Unhappy partners stop giving to their mates as soon as they sense they are no longer receiving. Happy partners don't take neglect so personally and believe that eventually their mate will show caring and consideration. In a happy marriage, it's important to learn to give even when you don't receive.

Have a "politeness week."[7] One spouse is to treat the other as if he/she were a special guest. (A good host is polite even when a guest is not.) Polite behaviors may include fixing breakfast; asking what the other person would like to watch on television; asking, "Can I get you anything?" as you leave the room to get yourself a snack; adjusting the room temperature; not being argumentative; and saying "Please," "Thank you," and "Excuse me." House guests are often treated with more consideration than family members. A "politeness week" makes you more aware of the small ways you can show more consideration.

Go the extra mile. Periodically (about once a week) ask your partner, "What is one thing I could today (or this week) that would make your day go a little easier or make you feel a bit more special?"[8] This is an opportunity for your mate to express wishes that might be more involved than the ones listed for "caring days." Some possible responses: "I'd like it if you could take the kids to the playground for a few hours so I can have some free time." Or, "I'd like you to be in a romantic mood one night—candles, wine, music—and let's go to bed early."

Everyone can fall into a self-absorbed rut. Taking time to ask your partner what would make him or her feel special can help you climb out of that rut.

Keep in Mind

- Happy marriages are not free from conflict, but the conflict is offset by mutual acts of kindness and respect and by positive feelings toward one's spouse.

- Good intentions are nice. But the road to a happy relationship is paved by genuine acts of desired love and caring.

● When you doubt your partner really cares about you, all of his positive acts are suspect. When you believe your partner cares about you, none of his inconsiderate acts are taken too personally.

● Behind most repetitive arguments is the concern of being cared for by your mate. You'll have a difficult time negotiating and solving problems when you seriously question the depth of your partner's caring.

● No one can chronically sacrifice their own needs to the relationship and still be happy. If you resent being the glue that holds the marriage together check to see if you've made too many "hidden compromises" (chapter 8).

● If you want to feel more "special," tell your mate ways he or she can act that would make you feel that way. He will probably appreciate the guidelines.

Did You Know . . .

. . . that marriages made to last are not always fifty-fifty propositions? In a survey of 351 couples married for at least fifteen years, the happiest among them agreed that "You have to be willing to put in more than you take out."[*] At any point in a marriage, such things as a serious illness, job loss, or career change may mean that one partner contributes 80 percent to the marriage for months on end. Happy couples can handle that and don't feel owed by the less-involved partner. They trust that in the long run (over months or years) the give-and-take will balance out. In contrast, dissatisfied partners have a "tit-for-tat" approach, one that virtually insures greater dissatisfaction. (In a 1988 study, spouses who were kind to one another, but only with an "I'll be nice if you are nice" attitude, broke up within five years.[#])

Are you and your mate willing to put in more than you take out of your relationship with little resentment? Chances are your marriage will last.

[*] Lauer, J. & Lauer, R. Marriages made to last. *Psychology Today*, June 1985, p.26.
[#] Filson, E.E. & Thoma, S.J. Behavioral antecedents of relationship stability and adjustment: a five year longitudinal study. *Journal of Marriage and the Family, 50,* 1988, 785-795.

Secret #15

A Committed Relationship

Do you lie in bed at night secure in your partner's commitment to you? Or do nagging doubts—her flirtatiousness, his aloofness—disturb your rest?

When commitment to a relationship is weakened, the amount of love and trust in the relationship is diminished. You may consider yourselves the best of friends, but remember this: friends aren't usually fully committed to one another (though they do care). If your best friend takes a job two thousand miles away, you may remain friends, but it's unlikely you'll pack up and relocate, too. If your best friend betrays you, or simply develops interests divergent from your own, you may stop spending much time together. In a committed relationship, that doesn't happen.

Only in a committed relationship can you risk being fully intimate. When you doubt your partner's degree of commitment, you may walk on tiptoe, trying not to disturb him. You'll start second-guessing him—saying and doing only those things you think he'll appreciate and love you for. But you won't be yourself. And you'll never know whether he's hanging around because he wants you or the image you've created.

When you doubt your own degree of commitment, you'll hold back from giving fully to the relationship. But your holding back can have negative consequences of its own—diminished intimacy, caring, and companionship—which can lower your happiness and further unravel your sense of commitment.

Should You Stay in An Unhappy Marriage?

Happy couples have a belief that the marriage is sacred and that one's partner is dependable. They don't view commitment as a "chain that inexorably binds people together despite intense misery, but rather as a determination to work through difficult times."[1]

"The thought of divorce never enters my mind," one man told me. "I'm not always happy with my wife. But that's when my commitment to her means something."

At first, commitment may well be a by-product of a satisfying relationship: partners commit *because* they are happy together. But thereafter commitment is a force of its own. Commitment leads to further happiness as much as happiness leads to further commitment.

You may make a commitment because a relationship is working. But then you must keep your commitment in order to keep your relationship working. Commitment is a promise to hang in there, to keep investing in the relationship despite boredom, hurt, or the uncertainty of it all. Commitment is an agreement to be unhappy once in a while.

How would you feel if your mate promised "I'll stay with you as long as . . ."? Or even worse: "I'll stay with you . . . until I change my mind." Some marriages, certainly, should end. We all deserve more from this life than remaining in a chronically unhappy relationship. But a commitment with a list of qualifiers is something less than a commitment. "What I wanted was a commitment," said one woman, disturbed by her fiancé's demand for a pre-nuptial agreement. "But what he gave me was a commitment with an asterisk."

If your marriage is falling apart, it's understandable that you might no longer fully commit yourself to it. At such times, as long as some shred of hope exists, it can be helpful to commit—not to the relationship but to working on improving the relationship. Choose a time-frame acceptable to each of you (one week, one month, six months) and devote yourself to marital improvement.

Commitment . . .

- Provides us with something to hold on to when so much else in this world seems so chancy and unpredictable.

- Is more than a promise. It is a devotion to that promise.

- Has value precisely because reasons will always exist not to honor it.

● Is a decision to love, and a decision to maintain that love despite obstacles.

It isn't easy remaining committed when your relationship hurts. But being able to withstand and resolve marital problems requires such a commitment.

What to Do
Do yourself and your spouse a favor: verbally state your commitment from time to time. (This need not be a formal renewal of vows, although that would be nice). If making changes to improve the relationship, do so with the clear statement that such changes reflect deeper commitment. Spouses often say, "I love you" or "I miss you" but rarely acknowledge "I'm committed to you." Once in a while, that's important to hear.

If you sense you are less committed to the relationship than your mate (but wish to be more committed) resolve to act *more committed one day at a time.* Before you fall asleep at night, and right after you awaken in the morning, tell yourself you will act *as if* you were a fully committed partner for that day. Don't make the mistake of waiting until you *feel* more committed before you *act* committed. There is no better way to generate stronger feelings than to act in ways consistent with those feelings. If you act uncommitted, you'll feel uncommitted.

If you are more committed to the relationship than your partner (and are worried and frustrated by his stance), devote more energy to activities outside of the relationship *that are personally fulfilling.* As psy-

---

Did You Know . . .
. . . that children of divorced parents have a higher probability of divorcing? There is no clear reason why, but the one that best fits the data is this: adults whose parents are divorced have a greater fear of making a full commitment.*

* Norval, Glenn & Kramer, Kathryn B. The marriages and divorces of the children of divorce. *Journal of Marriage and the Family, 49*, 1987, 811-825.

chologists remind us,[2] an over-focus on the marriage by the more committed partner can actually *lower* the other's commitment even more. The less-committed partner may feel pushed or smothered (and back away for more space), and will devalue the need for personal commitment because he is confident the other will never leave. Besides, if you are over-involved trying to get your mate to be more committed, you are probably under-involved in other important areas of your life.

Don't use commitment as a bargaining tool. Commitment is non-negotiable. Keep in mind these two "Nevers": NEVER make idle threats about separation or divorce. Even if your marriage is in trouble, flippant remarks of "Why keep trying, let's just end it" corrode the core of the relationship. NEVER sleep in separate beds as a way to punish your mate or display anger. Sleeping together is a privilege, highly symbolic of one's faith and commitment.

Make two lists: the events that would diminish your desire to remain committed (such as an affair), and the events that would sustain or strengthen your commitment. Discuss these with your mate. Determine whether you could take any steps in the coming week that would serve to strengthen your commitment. Understand that some reasons for commitment (such as financial security or security of the children) are not based on love alone.

Keep in Mind

- Commitment is always a decision to act that way.

- You can act committed without yet feeling committed.

- Commitment is not a one-time decision. It is ongoing. Every effort to work through a difficult time is really a decision to re-commit to the relationship.

- The more committed you are, the longer and harder you'll persist through tough times. Success rarely occurs without persistence.

Recognizing Your Role in a Problem

"My wife Kathy doesn't want to have sex," Alan said. "That's the problem. Oh, we'll have it once in a while, but it's always my idea and it's never frequent enough. What's wrong with her?"

After a full assessment of the problem, a major stumbling block to Alan and his wife having a satisfying sex life was revealed. Early on, Alan hadn't distinguished between the times when Kathy wanted to make love and when she wanted only affection. Kathy never spoke up about it, either. Consequently, she began making excuses to avoid sex, believing that Alan was "only after one thing." Her distancing just increased his desires and made it more likely that the next time they were affectionate he'd push for something more. Neither one recognized they were caught in a vicious cycle, a "marriage-go-round." The more he pursued, the more she distanced. The more she distanced, the more he pursued. Until they halted that cycle, their sexual relationship was destined to create misery.

Alycia and Mark had a different problem but a similar vicious-cycle pattern. When Mark disciplined his stepson, Danny, Alycia often felt Mark was too strict. Concerned about her son's adjustment to his new "father," Alycia often compensated for Mark's strictness by being lenient. When Mark observed Alycia being lenient, he viewed it as undermining his position as a parent. Hurt and angry, he'd be lenient with Danny until he couldn't bear it, then would clamp down somewhat harshly. Alycia would complain again of his strictness and the cycle repeated itself.

Marriage-Go-Rounds:
When Solutions Become Part of the Problem

Marital dissatisfactions persist not because of problems but because of the ways couples have tried to resolve their problems. Alycia thought the "problem" was Mark's strictness. But her solution (complaining to Mark and showing more lenience toward her son) aggravated the situation. Alan believed the "problem" was Kathy's avoidance of sex. But his solution (to show patience for a while then push more strongly for sex) made the problem worse.

Alycia's and Alan's "solutions" did make a kind of sense. In some other context they might have worked. Ironically, it is precisely because those solutions made sense that Alycia and Alan didn't consider abandoning them when the desired effects weren't forthcoming. Instead, they intensified their efforts (much like pressing harder on the accelerator when your car is stuck in the mud) and unwittingly made the problem harder to resolve.

Common examples where the cure prolongs the disease:

- A parent constantly forces his children to "share." Never having anything to call their own, the children become more greedy and withholding, causing the parent to demand more sharing.

- A husband dislikes disclosing his feelings and prefers "reason" to emotion. That frustrates his wife, who becomes emotional. Her emotionality alarms him and prompts him to reason with her while keeping his feelings to himself.

- A wife who thinks her husband is "hiding something" interrogates him and scrutinizes his behavior. He resents the scrutiny and becomes less talkative and more evasive, reinforcing her belief that he is hiding something from her.

- A husband, uncomfortable with conflict, avoids discussing an obvious marital problem with his wife, who is angered and hurt by his withdrawal. The tension between them mounts, and the husband withdraws further.

While it's common to lay most of the blame for a marital problem at your partner's feet, the truth is that marital difficulties are *reciprocal* in nature. That is, each of you acts and responds toward the other in a manner that perpetuates conflict or dissatisfaction. One way to tell whether you and your mate are trapped on a marriage-go-round is first to determine whether you have any opposing traits. Is one of you "responsible," the other "irresponsible"? Assertive/Unassertive? Boring/The life of the party? Tidy/Sloppy? Outgoing/Shy? Spontaneous/Planful? Do you devote time and energy trying to convert your spouse? If so, you are probably reinforcing the exact behaviors you want changed.

The Blame Game

Blaming is another vehicle for a marriage-go-round, for these reasons.

- Once a blamer labels a spouse (as lazy, insensitive, a sex maniac, etc.), he doesn't have to consider his own role in the problem. The blamed partner then feels unjustly criticized, and the battle lines are drawn.

- Blamers have a tendency to withdraw in contempt precisely at the time their spouse is willing to be responsive. Consequently, partners can't seem to work on the problem at the same time.[1]

- After a while, blamers see only the evidence that supports their negative beliefs about their partners, selectively ignoring evidence to the contrary.

Clearly the trick is to stop blaming one another and stop reapplying "solutions" to marital discord that don't work.

What to Do

State aloud (to yourself) your ongoing method of resolving a marital issue.[2] Examples:

"I complain to my wife that she's overweight so that she'll be motivated to exercise."

"I avoid having sex so he'll understand how angry I am."

"I mumble when he speaks to me so he'll give me quiet time alone."

"I avoid telling her how I really feel because I don't want to 'rock the boat.'"

Repeat your statement out loud five times. Now answer this: Is it working? If the answer is "no," try a different "solution."

If your attempted solutions to improve marital interactions have failed and your prescription for success is to intensify your efforts, stop right there. Then tell your mate exactly what you were doing, and why, and tell him you think you may have only made the problem worse.[3] Example: "I wanted some time alone to relax after work but I knew you wanted me to talk to you about your day. So I did my usual thing of going into the den without saying a word, hoping you'd get the message. Chances are though, I only made you feel neglected."

Such remarks open the door to a constructive discussion about how to get both of your needs met. The remarks are also non-accusatory, something your mate will appreciate.

Practice the art of relabeling. Most behaviors can be classified as negative or positive, depending upon your mood. Is your aloof husband avoiding you or is he *tired* or *preoccupied?* Is she boring or *content?* Stubborn or *clear about what he wants?* Overemotional or *sentimental?* Passive or *tolerant* of the way things are? Suspicious or *inquisitive?* Lazy or *unregimented?* Get the idea? Ask yourself whether you've ever done any of the behaviors you dislike your spouse doing. If you have, what were your reasons for acting that way? Chances are you'll see more merit in your behavior than when your partner behaves the same way. Give him the same benefit of the doubt.

Assume your partner is behaving in a way that she feels is appropriate and in everyone's best interest. (That's probably how she feels, anyway.) Visualize her acting in the way you dislike, but also *visualize yourself responding to her more kindly.* (Get a clear, strong image of yourself doing that.) How were you able to imagine yourself responding differently? You did so by changing your *thinking.* Ascribing benign or positive motives to your partner's actions may help you respond more constructively.

Think twice. If you believe you are being unfairly labeled or blamed, first *acknowledge any merit* to the complaints. No, you're not *always* insensitive to her feelings, but is there any merit at all in what she's saying? If so, admit it. Then you can point out where you disagree.

Predict exceptions to the rule.[4] You and your mate don't *always* act in an unproductive manner. Once in a while your "lazy" husband tidies up. Once in a while your "critical" wife is complimentary. Once in a while you and your mate have a peaceful evening despite a lousy day at the office. How come? Predict with your mate which upcoming scenarios you or he won't respond to in a problematic way, and what factors will help bring that about. Predicting exceptions to the rule makes each of you more aware of behavior patterns that once were automatic. Once aware, you are in a better position to change them.

Use numbers. If you've expended energy trying to get your mate to change certain behaviors, first rate from 1 to 10 how invested you believe your mate is in changing (a 10 means he or she is extremely motivated to change). Then rate the degree of investment you have in your mate changing. Rule of thumb: if you are more invested in (translation: anxious about) your mate changing than he or she is, change is less likely to occur. It would be like pulling dead weight. Better to determine what it is you hope to gain by your mate changing, then try to get that need met (at least partially) some other way. Chances are that your mate's reluctance to change was based partially on his feeling that you didn't understand his need not to change. Backing off may help him feel more understood and can actually increase his willingness to accommodate you.

Keep in Mind

- It is not your partner's negative behaviors per se that cause you difficulty. It is what you think about those behaviors that leads to your feeling troubled.

- If a solution didn't work despite an honest effort, "more of the same" won't work.

- Once you recognize your role in the continuation of a problem, you have something worthwhile to change.

- Partners locked in an ongoing struggle that's going nowhere have important things to say that they don't believe have been fully heard or understood.

- You are always at a disadvantage when you are more invested in someone changing than he is in changing.

Secret #17

Balancing Career and Family Roles

Barbara and Kent had read stories about dual-career couples struggling to manage their careers and a growing family at the same time. They understood that sacrifice, tolerance, and understanding were required. "No problem," they concluded. They viewed themselves as an "enlightened" and non-traditional couple, very much in love. Kent would play a major role in the child care, "obviously," and still be a successful vice-president of a brokerage house. "Obviously" Barbara had a right to devote time to her career as a university professor without feeling guilty about "neglecting" her children. They had it all planned.

Four years and two children later they were managing fairly well, to their credit. But matters hadn't evolved the way they'd intended.

"Kent doesn't help out at home as much as he said he would," Barbara complained.

"I *do* help out," Kent protested. "You're just not aware of all I do."

"What about shopping for the kid's clothes once in a while?" Barbara asked. "I've asked you many times to do that but you always have an excuse not to."

"The last time I shopped for clothes you disliked what I bought. I figured that if you have a clear idea of what to buy then you should buy it, rather than criticize me.

"Don't get the wrong idea," Kent said, turning to me. "We really do love each other. Our problem is juggling the 'Three C's': careers, chores, and children."

Juggling the Three C's: New Findings
When women began entering the work force in earnest, two beliefs

were prominent: that a working "Supermom"* was at risk for depression and exhaustion, and that husbands do not do their fair share of the child care load at home.

One of those beliefs is false.

Some of the recent research findings:

- Women most depressed were those unemployed who wanted to be employed. Women least depressed were those employed (who wanted to be) or unemployed (who wanted to be.[1])

- Employment is associated with improved mental health for women and *diminished mental health for the husbands of working wives.* (Husbands aged thirty-five to fifty are most at risk for depression or diminished self-esteem if they have working wives. This has nothing to do with their increased home responsibilities; men at that age seem to require more emotional support from their wives, which is less available when wives work.) A wife's satisfaction with employment was not due to escaping the "drudgery" of being a homemaker. The happiest were the working wives who also enjoyed housework.[2]

- Overall, husbands in dual-earner marriages do their fair share of household chores (or a little less). But men are less involved in child care. In particular, men are much less inclined to deal with "mundane but necessary" child care responsibilities such as getting up with a youngster in the middle of the night or leaving work early to tend a sick child or to visit a pediatrician.[3] Ironically, the wives in this study (women with professional careers) were very pleased with their husbands' performances in child care. But they were displeased with their own performance. "I'm not doing enough for my kids"

---

* By the way, "Supermom" is a term used to describe women who must do it all: manage career and home-life. With the rise of women's employment, men have had to take a shift, too. Without role models, today's husband has had to learn how to be a more involved parent and a homemaker, as well as provide financially for the family. Unlike many women, men typically do not have the option to stop working. We do not call such a man "Superman."

was their proclamation, despite the fact that they were doing more than their mates.

- In one-quarter of all two-income homes, the spouses work different shifts. In such households, couples have poorer health, less sleep, fewer friends, and less leisure time to spend with their mates. Their rate of divorce is slightly higher than the national average.[4]

- While some men may be depressed that their wives work, and while most working women enjoy working, dual-earner couples are as satisfied in their marriage as one-earner families.[5]

The Role of Socialization

According to researchers, men have been socialized to place "work" at the center of their lives, while "love" is at the center of a woman's.[6] Consequently, women do feel guilty when careers conflict with child care or home responsibilities. Men, however, believe that their job is their primary responsibility to their family. (Although most working women must work, for many women work is optional. Men generally have no option.) So a man who works overtime and misses his child's performance in the school play feels less guilt than his wife would. Working overtime is consistent with his view of being a responsible parent.[7]

Socialization accounts for these phenomena: when income is inadequate to meet expenses, men feel responsible—even if their wives have well-paying jobs. When something is wrong with a child (emotionally or physically), women feel responsible—even if their husbands are very involved in child care.

In a 1991 study, two hundred college students were asked to evaluate some fictitious women. Each woman was described as either divorced or married, with one child, and unemployed by choice—or employed in a low-, a moderate-, or a high-prestige job. The results? Married women were considered better adjusted than divorced women. Working women were viewed as "competent," but working mothers were regarded as less nurturing, less sensitive to others' needs, less dedicated to their family, and more selfish than non-working mothers.[8] Some attitudes are hard to shake off.

Balancing career and family roles is a challenge with more obstacles than answers. But improvements can still be made.

What to Do

Make a list (with your partner) of the chores and child care responsibilities you perform. Mark "A" if you "Always" do a specific task, "S" if the task is equally "Shared," or "I" if you do the task "Infrequently." Without blaming or criticizing, discuss which areas of responsibility you'd like changed. (For example, a husband might prefer his wife to trim the hedges more often. She might prefer him to do the grocery shopping more often.) For the time being, set aside areas of strong disagreement. Change only those items where there is mutual agreement.

Make a list of the ways you believe your partner could be more flexible in his or her job. (There is a tendency for couples to view their relationships as more flexible than their jobs. Consequently, they rarely adjust their work schedules and expect too much pliability from their marriage.) Negotiate one job-adjustment each for a limited time. Example: leaving for work later (or earlier) in the day to allow more time to spend with each other or with the children, or refusing overtime assign-

---

Did You Know . . .

. . . that men who worked longer hours and were most satisfied with their jobs had daughters with *lower* self-esteem?* In a recent study of 483 (mostly white) fifth through ninth graders, the more hours a man spent working, the less time he had available to his daughters, not to his sons. The reason is unclear, but it was speculated that men convinced themselves their daughters "needed a mother" and that their sons "needed a father."

Another study showed similar results but with an added surprise. Fathers with time-pressured jobs chose to spend more hours working if they had only a daughter. They worked fewer hours if they had only a son.[#] But surprisingly, mothers with complex and satisfying jobs were more warm and responsive to their sons than other mothers, but were not as responsive to their daughters as they were to their sons. Again, the researchers had no explanation but speculated that mothers believed their sons needed "more time to be socialized."

* Adler, Tina. Parents jobs linked to childrearing style. *APA Monitor*, Washington, D.C., September, 1991, p.9.

[#] Adler, Tina. Parents jobs linked to childrearing style. *APA Monitor*, Washington, D.C., September, 1991, p.9.

ments for two months. In one family, the husband had ten more days of vacation each year than his wife. Instead of taking those ten days off with little to do, he divided them into twenty half-days. Twenty times during the year he took a half-day off. He used the time to get caught up on chores, to be alone or occasionally with his wife, and to have the evening meal prepared by the time the rest of the family arrived home. It was a more productive use of his vacation time.

Make a pact that once a week for one month each of you (particularly the husband) will discuss one problematic or "challenging" part of his job for about fifteen minutes. Often, men are reluctant to discuss job difficulties, worried their wives will get upset or judge them as inadequate. Many wives feel shut out of their husband's work life. This task allows you to "try on for size" the option of talking about the challenges of your work.

Keep in Mind

- If there aren't enough hours in the day, reorganize. If that doesn't help, you have too much to do.

- Overall, once a couple has children, there is a drift toward more traditional values and roles within the family.[9] For some it is a welcome change; for others, a disconcerting one.

- The current generation has had few dual-earner role models. So working women have to find their own way to feel less guilt, and men have to find their own way to cope with their working wives being less available to them. Because of your efforts, the next generation may have it a bit easier.

Secret #18

Knowing You Can Trust

Trust is a keystone of a happy relationship.

Without trust you must hold back on intimacy in order to protect yourself. That keeps you on your guard, and also keeps you feeling lonely. Without trust you can't commit heart and soul to the relationship. Without intimacy, without commitment, what's left to hold your relationship together? Sexual attraction? Not for long.

"Why can't you trust me?"

Most people would respond by pointing to something the other person did that was hurtful or disloyal. "Because you cheated on me." "Because you lied to me." "Because when I needed you the most you were unavailable."

No doubt, partners can act in hurtful, disloyal, untrustworthy ways. But the truth, hard to swallow, is that rarely are there innocent victims.

Some people mistrust a partner because they've been badly hurt by others, and refuse to make themselves vulnerable again by fully trusting.

Some people mistrust a partner because they know they themselves are (potentially) untrustworthy. I've lied to you before, they think, so maybe you're lying to me now.

Some people mistrust as a way to avoid examining their own role in the relationship problem. "The problem is that he cheated on me. I didn't cheat on him." True. And cheating on a mate is a lousy, hurtful way to deal with an unsatisfying marriage. But when the betrayed spouse wonders how she can ever regain trust, one way is for her to focus on her role in the relationship problems. To the extent she can take an active role in changing hurtful patterns of interaction, she is no longer helpless and she increases the odds her mate will be faithful (and that she will be faithful).

The solution to regaining trust requires a bipartisan effort. Withholding trust until your partner "earns" it is a solution bound to complicate your life. Why? First, prolonged mistrust compels you to search for evidence of disloyalty or untrustworthiness, and to be suspicious of any positive thing he does. Consequently, you won't give him the benefit of the doubt and he'll feel constantly under fire and unappreciated for his sincere efforts to change. Second, if your mate resents your persistent mistrust, he may be slow to offer reassurances of his truthfulness. Tired of your scrutiny, he'll become evasive. Or, knowing that whatever he says won't be believed, he may add to the truth—saying what he thinks you want to hear—which only adds inconsistencies to his story and doubt to your beliefs.

The more you mistrust, the more you help create a context where there is reason to continue mistrusting.

Mistrusting is painful. Only a betrayed spouse can know how painful it is to have to doubt some act of kindness or consideration by a remorseful spouse. "Is he only doing that to appease me, or does he really mean it?" A betrayed spouse, even after a period of healing, of good times, is often "waiting for the other shoe to drop." Ironically, trustworthy and loving acts by a once untrustworthy partner, sometimes only add to the apprehension of when the next betrayal or act of deceit will come. "I trusted him once, until I discovered he'd been having a year-long affair. Now everything *appears* fine, but I was wrong once before . . ."

Learning to trust again in such a circumstance is difficult, but far from impossible.

A Faithful Spouse Is Not Just Monogamous . . .

. . . but is faithful to the commitment to love you as fully as possible. Your spouse need not betray you for trust to be in doubt. Ridicule, angry outbursts—anything that makes it difficult to expose yourself to your mate—kindle mistrust. Mistrust can surface in any context where one partner has less control or influence over an important marital item, such as money. Do you have little say over financial decisions? Does your partner keep his income a secret? Can one of you buy whatever you wish whenever you want, while the other must ask permission?

Do you feel controlled by your mate in any way? Does your partner insist on being right and blaming you when things go wrong? Do you believe him? If you do, you are probably very dependent on him for money or love and won't risk challenging him. But make no mistake, there is little trust.

Do you believe that people will take advantage of you if given the opportunity? Do your feelings get easily hurt? Do you feel that others let you down? Distrustful people often think like that.

Are you jealous? Degrees of jealousy are common in relationships. Jealousy becomes a problem when your mate is innocent but you are jealous of his other relationships, even those in the past. Insecure, you imagine he is rejecting you when he isn't. You test his love and devotion regularly, and chances are he's tired of it. When the truth of one's innocence does not matter under the scrutiny of a jealous mate, the innocent partner has nothing else to offer.

Jealousy is based on your view that you are replaceable. When you believe you have nothing special to bring to a relationship, you devalue your uniqueness and can't fathom why your mate would want to stay with you. What author and psychiatrist David Viscott calls the "jealousy cycle"[1] is a three-part pattern:

1. Possessing low self-worth, you worry about being rejected, abandoned, or replaced.

2. You then doubt your partner's love, which hurts him and eventually causes him to withhold love.

3. Feeling unloved, your self-worth diminishes and you worry about being rejected, abandoned, or replaced.

Trying to prove to your jealous mate that you are trustworthy is a tiresome, no-win task. Eventually you'll resent her lack of faith in you, and your resentment will only add to her doubt and anxiety. A key ingredient, according to David Viscott, is to refuse to withhold your love despite your anger. That means be patient and continually remind yourself that the problem is your partner's insecurity, not your untrustworthiness.

What to Do

If your spouse mistrusts you for a good reason, don't automatically offer reassurances of your renewed faithfulness even if you are totally sincere. Anything you say that smacks of "You shouldn't feel that way" (translation: "You should trust me"), is insensitive to her pain. Your insensitivity may be more troublesome to her now than whatever you first did to hurt her. Better to say, "I know I am trustworthy and will continue to act accordingly, but I don't blame you for doubting me."

If you are the betrayed spouse and need your partner to speak to you in the manner just described, tell him so. His usual efforts to persuade you to feel better may be insensitive, but chances are he's saying what he thinks is helpful and loving.

If you are jealous or are finding it difficult to trust your mate, show him compassion. Tell him, "I'm feeling mistrustful again. I know that hurts and frustrates you." He won't like that you're mistrustful or jealous, but he'll at least feel understood and cared about.

If you must interrogate a spouse who once betrayed you, do so in a scheduled, structured session. Unfaithful partners who want a second chance grow weary and frightened of surprise attacks from their wounded mates. Agree ahead of time to sit for a specified amount of time where you can question your husband on his past deeds. When the time is up, no more questioning until the next session. This allows you to enjoy each other's company (as much as possible) without fear that an impromptu inquisition might ruin your time together. If questions arise during non-scheduled discussion times, write them down and ask them at the next session.

Select a section of time during the day when you will act as if you trust your mate. If she arrives home a half-hour late, for example, ask her what detained her and *accept the answer as true.* If she offers affection, don't question her motives. If you think she'd like to go the health club to exercise, suggest she go. Simply respond as a trusting mate would. Trusting can never be a "sure thing." It is always a leap of faith, a willingness to risk having your trust betrayed. If you could somehow arrange to make it impossible for your spouse to deceive you without your knowing, you might rest easily but you'd have no trust.

Instead of making (more) accusations ("You lied to me when you told me you'd be at your office today"), discuss the feelings that prompted your accusations. Talking about what scares you, angers you, or worries you ("It scares me when I call your office and they tell me you're gone for the day") is not accusatory and gets to the more important issue.

If obsessive thoughts about a mate's untrustworthiness run your life, schedule time during the day to worry.[2] Trying to force yourself *not* to obsess is futile. Research shows that people who devote about fifteen to thirty minutes daily to obsessive thoughts gain more control over them. The thoughts will return at other times during the day, of course. At such times, calmly tell yourself you will pay attention to the thoughts at the scheduled time—not before—and then go on about your business. It can take three days before you are more adept at this. But it is a strategy that works.

If you are eager to be more trusting but are struggling to do so, try this: lie on your back and allow your partner to lift your head an inch or two from the floor. Your job is to relax and let your mate support your head with no assistance from you. *This will take time.* Don't be concerned if you couldn't relax fully in your first few attempts. It's okay to switch places. If your partner has a hard time fully trusting you to support his head, he'll better understand how much more difficult it must be for you to fully trust him.

Did You Know . . .

. . . that a trusting person is no more gullible or naive than anyone else, and is probably better adjusted?* Trusting people are viewed by others as happier than distrusting people. Trusting people are less likely to lie or cheat and more likely to give someone a second chance. Distrustful people are more likely to cheat, if the opportunity presents itself, and less inclined to give someone a second chance.

Want more friends? People are more interested in being friends with a trusting person than a distrusting person.

* Nowinski, Joseph. *A Lifelong Love Affair: Keeping Sexual Desire Alive in Your Relationship.* New York: W.W. Norton, 1989, p.48.

Keep in Mind

- You can't be open and intimate with a spouse who demeans you. You can't trust if you can't be open.

- Don't wait until you feel trusting before you start trusting.

- Trusting is, by definition, a leap of faith. When you are 100 percent certain of something, trust is not required.

- If you suspect something is wrong, say so. You don't have to be accusatory to state your concerns.

Uncovering Hidden Agendas

"They're *my* parents, Gina. I don't want to visit them. I don't want to call them. We've been over this a dozen times already. Can't you just drop it?"

"I still don't understand why you won't even call your mother on her birthday, Lee. You've hardly spoken with her in five years. Don't you think it's time *somebody* put aside their pride . . ."

"Why can't you stay out of this?" Lee interrupted. "I told you, they're my parents, not yours. I don't tell you how to run your relationship with your parents, so why do you insist on running my relationship with my parents?"

"That's just it," Gina said. "You don't have a relationship with your parents. Can't you see that?"

"This is going nowhere," Lee concluded, walking out of the room.

Repetitive "Here we go again" arguments, standoffs, and stalemates happen, but not for the reasons people think. Lee believed that if Gina would just view the problem from his perspective, she'd back off. (Then again, if she was just being stubborn, maybe he should be stubborn, too. That would show her.) But the problem wasn't Gina's lack of understanding or her stubbornness. And the problem, despite what Gina believed, wasn't Lee's relationship with his parents. The real reason Lee and Gina argued periodically about this problem—to no avail—was because they weren't arguing about what they thought they were arguing about. Misidentifying the fundamental problem made it impossible to resolve.

Uncovering the Hidden Agenda

"What worries you about Lee's unwillingness to speak to his parents?"

I asked Gina one day.

"They are his parents. A son shouldn't simply cut himself off from his parents no matter what they've done to him," Gina answered.

"But how does his decision to cut himself off from his family affect you personally?" I probed.

"It doesn't," she began. "But . . . maybe I worry that if he can close himself off from his parents, he'll close himself off from me one day. Let's face it, we began marriage counseling because we've drifted apart the past two years."

"So it sounds to me that the reason you argue with him about his relationship with his parents is because it symbolizes something more important—his relationship with you. Deep down, you worry that he might stop loving you, too."

"Yes, that's right," she said.

"I never realized that before," Lee commented.

Lee never realized it because it was hidden. Hidden agendas crop up from time to time in a relationship. But for happy couples the hidden agendas don't stay hidden for long.

Hidden agendas begin as doubts or fears one spouse has about the other's level of commitment or caring. Examples:

SPOUSE A: "Let's ask the Pattersons to join us for dinner."

SPOUSE B: (The Pattersons? Doesn't she want to spend time alone with me?)

SPOUSE A: "We can't afford a piano. Besides, you know I've been waiting years to buy a backyard pool."

SPOUSE B: (He always gets his own way. Don't my wishes count?)

SPOUSE A: "Goodnight."

SPOUSE B: (Already? I thought we'd have time to chat before going to bed. Isn't he interested in knowing how my day went?)

SPOUSE A: "Dear (cough), would you bring me the vaporizer (gag), please?"

SPOUSE B: (She can't fool me. Her cold isn't that bad. That's just her way of avoiding sex.)

Hidden agendas, as you can see, are the undercurrents to a superficial dialogue. One problem with hidden agendas is that they are believed, and additional evidence is then gathered to support the belief. So if a husband believes his wife is avoiding sex with him, many of her (innocent) behaviors will be interpreted by him as avoidance. ("She wants to phone her sister? I've heard that excuse before . . .") Left unspoken, hidden agendas build hurt and frustration and couples end up arguing over seemingly unimportant matters.

"Why must you always call your sister!"

"What? I don't always call my sister. And it's a local call, so what's the big deal?"

The big deal is the meaning he gives to his wife calling her sister. But that meaning (his fear that she's avoiding sex with him), if left hidden, will complicate their relationship unnecessarily.

Three Kinds of Hidden Agendas

Researcher John Gottman and associates say that hidden agendas are about three fundamental issues:[1]

1. *Caring.* Does my spouse care about me? Love me? Trust me?

2. *Interest.* Is my mate interested in my thoughts, feelings, wishes? Is my mate responsive to me? Am I sexually appealing? Does he or she value my opinions? Can I talk to him or her about my future goals?

3. *Status.* Am I in a one-down position to my mate? Do his or her needs always come first? Do I have a say in important decisions?

Whether you're arguing about money, children, in-laws, or what to eat for dinner, if you're fighting that same old fight, then hidden agendas may be lurking.

What to Do

Call a "Time-Out" during a tiresome argument and try to determine your hidden agenda. Ask each other, "Are you worried or hurt because I'm not showing you enough love or caring? Are you hurt because I'm not taking an interest in you? Are you hurt because you feel controlled or powerless?" Once uncovered, allow the one with the hidden agenda to speak uninterrupted. Don't challenge or debate his or views. Every thirty seconds or so, summarize what you've heard to be sure you've understood correctly. If you respond to your partner's uncovered agenda with anger, insensitivity, or impatience, you'll fuel the original fear (fear of being unloved, uncared for, or controlled).

Send a signal. If you have difficulty revealing your hidden agenda during conversations or arguments, have a prearranged signal that will indicate to your spouse how you really feel. For example, a pillow placed outside and on top of the bedspread may signal that you are wondering if your partner finds you attractive or is interested in things important to you. A lighted candle may signal your doubts about being loved and cherished. Such symbols make your feelings known in a quiet but effective way, without accusation, and reflect your continued desire to improve the relationship.

Once your hidden agenda is revealed, agree with your mate that for the next two weeks you will call attention to behavior that sparks your hidden agenda. For example, if your agenda has to do with status and equal power in the relationship, inform your spouse every time you believe she is doing something that lowers your status. (You will notice those behaviors anyway. Calling attention to them gives your mate immediate feedback about his behavior and reduces the odds your resentment will build.) The purpose is not to debate whether or not you are right and your mate is wrong. The goal is to clarify when your hidden agendas are being sparked so that the two of you can work together with understanding.

Keep in Mind

- Arguments over "little things" are about bigger agendas.

- The three kinds of hidden agendas (caring, interest, and status) reflect fundamental needs in life: the need for love, self-esteem, and control (influence). Once uncovered, treat those needs with respect.

- You can help your mate uncover his or her hidden agendas by being less defensive when they are pointed out. Remember, revealing a hidden agenda is not an accusation. It is an explanation of one's feelings.

Remaining Connected to Your Original Family

Did you ever wish that your family was the inspiration for a Norman Rockwell painting? Imagine everyone, full of love and merriment, warming their hands in front of the hearth on a snowy Christmas day. The children—decorated with hot-cocoa mustaches—dart about the country home like rabbits. Friends drop by bearing cookies and fruitcake, shaking the snow from their coats. You can almost smell the turkey and the minty, evergreen wreath; you can almost hear the laughter, the crumpling of the wrappings, the chorus of *Jingle Bells*; everything and everybody mixing together as smoothly as hot butter into cream . . .

Well, maybe next year.

As appealing as it may be, most of us would be grateful for much less during the holidays. Appreciative children, a friendly phone call, a small but festive meal together, Bing Crosby. We don't ask for much, and often we don't even get that.

Holidays are special times for families, made complicated when family relationships are strained. When warm embraces and hot toddies are replaced by forced smiles and bickering, well, you can feel grateful when the whole damn day is over and done with.

But leaving your parents and siblings behind after a hard day of Christmas won't make you more content with life. Unresolved family issues stay with you and keep you discontented. You can't resolve those problems by ignoring them or living far away from them.

Family Affairs

When did you first feel grown up? After graduation? When you got married? After receiving your first paycheck from a "real" job? Those may be indications of adulthood. But two indications of maturity are. first, viewing your parents realistically—not as perfect, not as totally toxic—but as people with their own strengths and weaknesses. When you can view your parents as they are, not as they once were or how you'd like them to be, you've grown up a bit more. A second indication of maturity is the ability to be true to yourself (and less anxious) in your family's presence. That means being able to say "yes," "no," and "ouch." It means no longer pretending that all in the family is okay if it is not okay.

When you get married, it's important to distance yourself from your parents and family somewhat. I'm not talking escape or avoidance. I'm referring to the natural need to bond with your mate, to have room to grow, to become a cohesive twosome, independent from your original families. Remaining connected to your family of origin is important (particularly if you have a supportive, caring family), but the real work is to consolidate your relationship with your spouse. Once that is accomplished (and it could take several years), you reconnect to your family in a different way—less as a son or daughter, more as an adult. Couples on the extreme—either too involved with their original families, or too disconnected—will eventually have problems.

Janine came from a "close" family. The three grown daughters had such a positive relationship with their mother that they kept nothing from her. No secret, no marital issue, no personal problem was private where Mom was concerned. Dad loved them too, but of course he was a man, on the periphery of the family, involved in masculine endeavors. What did he know?

The family problems were many. Mom and Dad had a polite relationship, but that was all. Mom confided in Janine often about her lonely life with Dad ("If I didn't have you to talk with, Janine, I don't know what I'd do"). After Janine married, her husband Mike had all he could do to convince her to live in an apartment. She wanted them to live with her parents (to save money, of course). Within a year, Mike had grown tired of the many nights they spent at Janine's parents. Weekends were especially difficult. Sunday afternoons were reserved for her family, and that was that. So Mike did what any red-blooded American boy would do. He took up golf. Soon Janine spent more time confiding in Mom about her faltering relationship with Mike than she spent with Mike. Shortly before their third anniversary, Mike and Janine separated.

In Janine's case, having a close family choked off her relationship with her husband.

Will had a different relationship with his parents. None. He wanted as little to do with them as possible, and he had good reasons. So when he married Rochelle, all was wonderful for a while. But Will's problem was his ambivalence about being close to someone. In one sense, he felt very needy for love, trying to fill the hole left open by his uncaring parents. But he also was frightened of too much closeness. After all, the closer you get, the more deeply you could be hurt. With Rochelle, he'd demand closeness; sensitive to the slightest rejection on her part yet indifferent to her needs. He gave and took, but only on his terms.

Disconnecting yourself from your original family—even for understandable reasons—often leaves you hungry for love but unwilling to expose yourself to being hurt. Your relationships move in fits and starts, never satisfying for long, thereby increasing your need for—and fear of—love.

If you've been hurt by your parents, disconnecting from them for a period of time can be a useful and necessary step in the process of healing. Confrontations may also be necessary. But resolution doesn't happen if you are held prisoner by your anger. Your parents may never change. They may never understand your hurt. They may never express remorse. But totally disconnecting from them, or connecting with them only in anger, won't heal you or make you feel closer to your mate.

If you are too close or too distant from your parents, your goal is to connect with them, to be in emotional contact with them without struggling to change them. That means you must let them be who they are. You don't have to like it. You don't have to put up with it. ("Dad, if you're going to keep criticizing me, I'm going to hang up. I hope you feel better next time.") But you do have to accept the way things are. You may have to grieve that your relationship with them will never be better than it already is. You deserved more from your parents, and they failed you in some important way. That's unfair. That's sad. And that's reality. When you let go of your unmet expectations of your parents, you can get on with your life more happily and productively.

What to Do

Focus less on what a parent does to bother you and pay more attention to how you respond.[1] Think of what happens between you and your parent as a dance. It takes two of you to keep the dance going. Changing your response to a parent's predictable ways can help alter the dance pattern. How do you ordinarily respond? Rehearse a different response. If confrontation never helped, ignoring provocative behaviors might (but stay consistent—ignoring one unkind remark but exploding after the fifth is not a significant change). If you always debate your parent, try listening with empathy ("Sounds like you're feeling hurt, Mom.") Even if your response doesn't work the way you'd like, your main goal is to respond less automatically and with more thought. It is your knee-jerk reactions (even if they are non-verbal) that need altering. Don't defend yourself against unfair accusations or subtle criticisms. Responding, "I'm sorry you feel that way" or "That's interesting" keeps you balanced and in control.

Connect with each parent (or sibling) separately. On the telephone, be sure to talk with each parent. (One parent being the spokesperson for both can add distance to your relationship with the other.) In person, try to arrange for time alone with each parent or sibling. Take a walk with your father. Help Mom prepare a meal. Connecting with family members only as a group diminishes one-on-one intimacy.

Limit conversations about an absent family member. When relationships are strained, there is a tendency to converse with a parent about *other* family members instead of keeping the focus only on the two of you. Some discussion of others is normal. But take time to ask "How are *you* doing?" and don't get sidetracked.

If the relationship with one or both parents is highly conflicted, and reasonable "adult" dialogues go nowhere, write a letter to the parent detailing your hurt and anger. Be as specific as possible, but don't mail it. It provides some cathartic relief, clarifies your issues, and can better prepare you for any future discussions. A letter of this kind can be especially helpful if a parent is deceased.

To better understand your parents, talk to your aunts and uncles about them. (Holidays and birthdays are convenient times to do this.) Ask them what it was like for your parents when they were growing up. Don't complain to a relative, especially if you believe that relative will inform your parents. Indirect messages are not helpful.

Don't agree to keep secrets if doing so divides your family loyalty. (Except for a surprise birthday party, it is *never* a good idea to agree to keep a secret from your mate.) According to family therapist Edwin Friedman,[2] secrets disrupt family communication and worsen pre-existing problems. (Common secrets include health issues, pregnancies, affairs, financial woes, etc.) Since only some family members are "in" on the secret, they have to speak cautiously around those "not in" on the secret. Having to pre-think what they say so they won't inadvertently "spill the beans" makes conversations stilted. Secrets only add to anxiety. Consequently, pre-existing problems worsen as the anxiety level elevates. While you might be intrigued by family gossip, never promise to keep secrets that will make you uncomfortable. If someone tells you a secret before you have a chance to protest, you don't have to keep the secret if it makes you uncomfortable. That the secret-teller's problem, not yours.

Refusing to keep secrets is disruptive to the family at first. But it helps keep you sane.

Keep in Mind

- Staying connected to your family does not mean putting up with abuse. You can detach—as much as you need to to protect yourself—but still remain connected.

- We usually expect our partners to make up for what we didn't get growing up. Since our partners are not responsible for our happiness, we'll eventually blame them for our discontent.

- Forgiving a parent is good and healing, but may not be your next step. Recognizing your anger and hurt and seeing its merit, rather than pretending you shouldn't feel the way you do, must occur first.

- You can't divorce your parents.

Secret #21

Taking Time for Yourself

"What are we having for supper tonight?"

"Where are we going this weekend?"

"We need to spend more time together."

"When should we visit your parents?"

"What should we say to Jeffrey about his report card?"

We, we, we. Being married certainly is a "we" proposition. And when kids enter the picture, whatever sense of privacy or self you enjoyed goes down the drain faster than Ninja Turtle soap suds. But remaining happily married requires an "I" focus, too.

Is taking time for yourself a selfish preoccupation? It can be if you routinely neglect the needs of others. But one of the more selfish things you can do is to neglect yourself. Why? Because when you neglect yourself you become needy. You then require more help from others and resent it when help isn't forthcoming. Selfishness can unravel a relationship. But so can an absence of selfishness.

Who were you before you became a "we"? Does any part of that person still exist? When you're alone (do you have quiet time to be alone?) who is the "me" inside of you?

"My teenager was talking about his future dreams," a middle-aged man told me one day. "He wants to become an actor. An actor, can you believe it? He explained to me—before I could warn him myself—that 95 percent of all actors are unemployed and he doesn't care. He simply wants to act. You know what? I envy him. Not for his wish to be an actor. I envy him because he has a dream."

Look Inward, Angel

People stop dreaming when they think it's time to wake up. Mortgages, taxes, children, aches and pains, hair loss, a fondness for quieter music—are all reminders that you're older now and that the real world must be faced, not an imaginary one. But if facing the real world means abandoning personal dreams or losing your sense of individuality, you may feel imprisoned by your commitments and smothered by your intimate relationships.

Happy couples not only balance time together with time apart, they use their individual time to replenish themselves. "The prevailing pattern for managing time," according to author Frederic Hudson, "is to work most of the time, to love some of the time, and to do fantastic things on weekends—[which] leaves people feeling their lives are little more than the shadows of their jobs."[1] Self-renewal is more than collapsing into your favorite chair to watch sitcoms on television. Without self-renewal, a spouse often believes his partner should fill the void in his life. Should that partner fail in filling the void (which is inevitable), the spouse disengages somewhat from the marriage, knowing "something is missing" but falsely presuming that the "something" is marriage-related, rather than self-related.

Broadly, there are two kinds of self-renewal. Taking time to do more of those things you really enjoy is one type. Vacations sometimes serve that purpose, though most people could use more than the allotted two weeks every summer. Learning to relax, to enjoy solitude, to gaze at a night sky and feel a stirring of wonder and peace—all help you to reorient yourself to your neglected inner world.

A second level of self-renewal is more profound and longer lasting. It involves having a vision for your life, a mission or purpose. Too many people with worthwhile dreams talk themselves out of them. They convince themselves that they already have too many responsibilities. Besides, dreams are risky. But meaningful dreams, according to Frederic Hudson, are not items on a wish list but "a visceral yearning . . . a picture of what you most deeply want your life to count for . . . a haunting refrain . . ."[2] Will your dream still be important a year, or five years, from now? When your life is nearing its end, will you regret your decision to forsake that dream? If you answered "Yes," you have a dream worth pursuing.

"I've thought about doing it for years," Claudia said wistfully. "I love horses. I owned a horse when I was a teenager. My dream is to own and operate a large stable, to care for other people's horses—as well as one of my own. I'm afraid to talk to Tom about it, though. What if he hates the idea? Maybe I should forget the whole thing. Shouldn't I?"

Maybe. Maybe not. If your dream makes you apprehensive, join the club. Dreams challenge us to stretch our capacities, which increases the risk of failure or setbacks. If you abandon your dream, will you resent your spouse for "holding me back"? If so, you are not accepting full responsibility for your decision. Instead, you are holding your partner responsible.

Henry's dream was to entertain. He was married with two kids and had a secure job as a computer programmer, but he also sang well and played a mean piano. He never followed his dream and blamed his wife. True, she didn't like the idea that as an entertainer he'd spend his weekends in clubs rather than at home. But he never took the time to tell her how important his dream was to him. He never bothered to listen to her concerns with compassion and without complaint. He never tried to negotiate with her in a way that might meet both their needs. His dream was his responsibility, but he never understood that.

Sometimes a person lets go of a dream in order to commit more strongly to the marriage dream (for example, by turning down a promotion that would have required spending too much time away from home). A sacrifice, to be sure, but done for a worthwhile reason—to allow the marriage to flourish. It's not always easy to know which dream should be followed and which should fade. But happy couples keep dreams alive.

Have you given up a bit of yourself over the years? Do you often think in terms of "we" or "us" and rarely "I"? If so, you're preventing your spouse from enjoying a major source of marital pleasure: a partner who likes himself, enjoys himself, and who has personal goals and ambitions.

What to Do

Respond to this statement: If I had complete freedom (more opportunity, more money, support from my spouse, etc.) I'd probably devote more time to . . . . If you come up with an answer that you can't shake off, you owe it to yourself to take the idea seriously.

Make a list of twenty activities you'd enjoy doing by yourself over the next several months: taking in a few matinees, exercising, reading more spy novels, taking nature photos, going to a bar with friends, canoeing, fishing, taking a class on flower arranging, getting a babysitter for an afternoon while you go to a museum. Now start doing some of them. At a minimum try two per month.

To improve your motivation, keep the list posted in a prominent place. Every time you do an activity, place a check-mark next to that item on your list. Ask your mate to encourage you. If one of the items listed is extremely special but too difficult or expensive to do regularly (taking a weekend trip, attending a Broadway play, dining at a five-star restaurant, etc.), use that as a reward for accomplishing a specific number of the smaller activities.

For three days, note all *of your activities and how much time you devoted to each.* Finding time for self-renewal often requires curtailing other activities. Can you eliminate a half-hour of television daily? For a few months can you get in the habit of tidying up the children's toys only once a day (perhaps just before bedtime) instead of doing it as often as you ordinarily do? Can you make creative use of your lunch hour? (Picnic in the park, exercise, listen to music from a portable tape player, etc.?) Prioritize. Are you spending too much time on less satisfying activities? If so, can you rearrange priorities, even for just a few weeks?

Build a dream. Devote at least fifteen minutes a day, four days a week, for one month to quiet introspection. If relaxing background music adds to the atmosphere, fine. Contemplate a dream for your future. You'll know you've hit pay-dirt when the vision excites you, gives you a burst of energy, and stays with you when your fifteen minutes are over. Once the dream is clear, what is the first thing you could do to help make that dream an eventual reality? The second thing? Obviously, you don't have to act on your dream immediately, but focusing on the necessary and challenging steps required to make your dream a reality can boost your motivation.

Keep in Mind
- Whether you abandon a dream or "go for it," the responsibil-

ity for the decision is totally yours.

- Taking time to renew yourself can be one of the nicest things you can do for your partner, too.

- The failure to be selfish once in a while can render you needy, helpless, or demanding—which will only make you more selfish.

Secret #22

Knowing When to Keep Quiet—and When Not to

"So there we were having dinner when this waiter came by and said . . ."

"No, dear," Lynn interrupted. He wasn't a waiter, he was the manager."

"Whatever," Al said. "Anyway, this waiter or manager asks us if we were the couple that complained about the prime rib. I told him 'No,' but before he left . . ."

"Not exactly, dear. We were eating prime rib. But the manager asked if we complained about our *meal*. He never actually said *prime rib*."

"It doesn't matter," Al griped. "The point I'm trying to make . . ."

"Wait 'til you hear this, you'll love it," Lynn said to their guests. "Go ahead, Al. Finish the story."

Talking is fine but the art of biting your lip is equally important to learn.

Clearly, Lynn was impolite to keep interrupting her husband in front of their guests. But should Al have spoken up about it? In this case, yes, because he was irritated with her the rest of the evening.

"Why didn't you ask me to stop interrupting you?" Lynn queried later on.

"Because I was being polite," said Al. "I didn't want to embarrass you in front of your friends."

That was thoughtful of Al. But Lynn paid for his thoughtfulness by having to put up with an annoyed husband the rest of the evening. Maybe it wasn't so thoughtful of him after all.

If you informed your spouse every time he or she did something that annoyed you, you might not help matters. "Why are you so nitpicky?" would be a common response to your openness. Overlooking petty annoyances is one of the unwritten rules of a happy marriage. But overlooking too many annoyances won't keep you happy for long. Keep quiet or speak up. Where do you draw the line?

Guidelines

If you keep quiet about some issue, will you resent your mate later? If so, speaking up is the wiser course of action.

Couples who err on the side of keeping quiet do so for reasons they feel are important. Like Al, some partners justify their silence by saying it's "polite." Being polite is nice, but some people confuse unassertiveness with politeness. (One way to tell whether you are being polite, not unassertive: politeness makes you feel good; unassertiveness leaves you feeling tense.) Some don't speak up because they fear it will make matters worse. (And it might. But pent-up feelings take

---

Did You Know . . .

. . . that some couples routinely keep quiet about issues to avoid an argument? "Conflict-avoidant" couples are less happy over the long-term than "conflict-engaging" couples. (Over the short-term, conflict-engagers are less satisfied.) Still, even happy couples choose to avoid conflict once in a while. How can you tell if you and your mate are primarily conflict-avoiders? Research findings suggest you consider the following guidelines.* Conflict-avoiders:

- Don't often discuss routine topics, such as how their day went.
- Don't view their partners as resources to turn to when they are feeling blue.
- Don't expect their mate to be their friend. (Consequently, they feel lonelier.)
- Don't see their role in a problem. Instead they feel their partner is to blame.
- Often hold a strong, traditional view of sex-roles.
- More often are male.

If you think you are a conflict-avoider, chances are that your decision to keep quiet about some issues is founded more on anxiety than caring. Speaking up will create tension in the short run but may ultimately make your marriage more satisfying.

* Gottman, John. How marriage changes. In Gerald R. Patterson's (Ed.) *Depression and Aggression in Family Interactions*. Hillsdale, N.J.: Laurence Erlbaum Associates, 1990.

their toll on the individual and the relationship, too.) Some don't speak up out of a sense of futility. It won't make a difference, they believe. In general, if keeping quiet is motivated by negative feelings (fear, helplessness, guilt, etc.), the long-term results will be negative (resentment, diminished caring). If keeping quiet is motivated by love or consideration, chances are it will help the relationship thrive.

What to Do

If unsure whether to speak up or keep quiet, postpone your decision. If any discomfort or negative feeling persists, that's a sure sign to talk about it. If the feeling hasn't gone away by keeping it to yourself, more withholding won't help.

Before you speak up, answer this question: What do I wish to get out of this discussion? Sometimes the matters we bring to our partner's attention are symbols for some hidden agenda. Telling your spouse she is too angry with the children may be a cover for your concern that she is unhappy with you. Best to ignore the children issue and raise the question of how the two of you are doing. What else might you really want from the discussion? Do you feel like starting an argument? Why? Do you just feel like chatting? How about reporting *that* instead of whatever (potentially hazardous) issue you may have thought about raising?

Take a "speak up hour." If you and your mate have too many petty criticisms of each other (or, if you rarely complain but wish you were more assertive), schedule a "speak up hour" once a week. The rule is that each of you is allowed to express your annoyance about things you might otherwise ignore. Don't make pejorative comments ("You're lazy"). Instead, say "I'd prefer it if you would . . ." The structure of a scheduled discussion helps eliminate off-the-cuff complaints during the remainder of the week. (Review chapters 2 and 3 to help minimize defensiveness and improve communication during this exercise).

When trying to let go of some petty criticism of your mate, envision your partner wrapped in a white light.[1] Often, such an image softens your perception and makes it easier to regard some issues as "No big deal."

If unsure when to speak up or stay silent, ask your mate for the guidelines he would like you to follow. It can be helpful to know in which situations your mate would prefer you'd speak up, and in which situations he'd prefer you not speak up. You may not agree with what he says (you don't have to agree), but you might find it informative. The rules to follow for the problem of when to keep quiet are flexible, so whatever works best for the two of you is fine.

Keep in Mind

- Ignoring petty annoyances is an unobservable act and therefore goes unnoticed by spouses. Pat yourself on your back for your efforts (and realize that your partner has ignored some of your annoying habits, too).

- If you choose to speak up, do so without being harsh or accusatory.

- Uncertain what to do? Determine what you believe was your partner's deepest motive for doing what he did. If his motive was benign or positive, choose to keep quiet. You can raise the issue later if you think you were mistaken.

Secret #23

Loving It Up with Sex and Affection

Want a sex life to match that of the happiest couples? Well, jumping into bed together more often won't suffice. While it's true that happily married partners are very satisfied with their sexual relationship, it's not because they "do it" more often. Actually, sexual experimentation is more important to happy couples than frequency of sex.[1] But the most important source of marital happiness has to do with the character of one's spouse. According to a major national survey, a spouse who makes you feel important, who is kind, gentle, exciting, and good with children—*and* who is sexually satisfying and prone to sexual experimentation—most powerfully influences your marital satisfaction.

So how do you best add zest to your love life? First, enhance your appeal as a spouse by having more intimate conversations and by showing more consideration and non-sexual affection. *Then* add some novelty and creativity to your lovemaking (use body oils, erotic play, try different positions—anything out of the ordinary will do). It's a formula that works.

"Doctor, My Wife Wants a Trapeze Installed in Our Bedroom. Is That, Uh, Normal?"

A trapeze is not a common bedroom accoutrement. But what is common is for husbands to underestimate the amount of interest their wives have in sex. (Nearly 100 percent of romance novels are read by women. Most romance novels contain highly erotic passages.) Women fantasize about sex as intensely as men, though less frequently. In fact, for women over forty, engaging in acts of "sexual abandon" with their mate makes them feel more attractive and appealing.[2] By being more communicative, considerate, and affectionate, husbands can tap into the sexual energy their wives already possess.

Also uncommon is for wives to fully understand what the act of making love means to their husbands. To believe that their husbands "are only after one thing" misses something fundamental. Men may "know" they are loved by their wives, but they *feel* loved when they make love. Husbands who complain they aren't getting enough sex may really be feeling they aren't getting enough love.

What is "normal" when it comes to sexual satisfaction may surprise you. A report from the *New England Journal of Medicine* revealed that 20 percent of wives and one-third of husbands from satisfying marriages reported current dissatisfaction with their sexual relationship.[3] (Researchers studied one hundred educated couples with an average age of thirty-three.) Forty percent of the men in the study reported occasional erectile or ejaculatory problems. Sixty-three percent of the women reported difficulties with arousal or orgasm (coming too quickly or not quickly enough). Half of the men and 77 percent of the women reported an occasional lack of interest in sex. The frequency of intercourse averaged once a week (one-third reported having sex less than once a week; 10 percent had sex less than once a month). Evidently, mild sexual frustrations and occasional loss of sexual interest are par for the course even in happy marriages.

Why Affection Is So Important

In 1953 Miss Sweden was five feet, seven inches tall and weighed 151 pounds. In 1983 Miss Sweden was five feet, nine inches tall and weighed 109 pounds.[4] Affection has always been an important feature of a loving marriage. But in a world where standards of physical attractiveness fluctuate, a person needs to know she is still attractive to her mate or he to his mate. Regular shows of affection help.

Americans are obsessed with their appearance. About 40 percent of men and 50 percent of women are quite dissatisfied with their weight or their mid-torso.[5] In a study of five hundred children, half of the girls claimed they were overweight (in fact, only 15 percent were overweight).[6] About thirty million men (and most men over age fifty) develop male-pattern baldness. According to Thomas Cash, researcher at Old Dominion University, when hair starts to thin, so does a man's self-esteem.[7] One-third of men with modest hair loss are more sensitive to criticism, envious of good-looking men, and worried about their appearance.

Having a warm, loving spouse who demonstrates affection regularly can calm the fears associated with "losing your looks."

Affection doesn't just make you feel better; it may even prolong your life. Early child care studies showed that children in orphanages who were properly fed but not held or cuddled died at an alarming rate. One study was originally designed to test how a high cholesterol diet affected heart disease in rabbits. Initial results were confusing until the researchers discovered a flaw in the experiment. Evidently the person whose job it was to feed the rabbits also petted and handled those rabbits whose cages were within reach. The petted rabbits showed a 60 percent reduction in heart disease compared to non-handled rabbits, despite a high-cholesterol diet.[8]

An affectionate spouse tells you that you are loved and desired despite a sagging body or cranky disposition. Showing affection is a way of caring, of soothing the bumps and bruises of everyday life. Everybody needs a hug.

In all, happy couples aren't sexual acrobats or insatiable lovers. But when it comes to sex they are thoughtful, creative, patient, and enthusiastic lovers. You can be, too.

What to Do

For one month, be affectionate with your mate eight to ten times a day. It needn't be passionate. If there have been arguments lately about sex, be sure your shows of affection are non-sexual. Caress his back as you pass by him in the kitchen. Squeeze her hand. Kiss him on the cheek. Rub her shoulder. Sexual displays of affection (such as pinching his bottom) are fine if your mate is receptive, but the goal of this exercise is to be affectionate without it necessarily leading to sex. (This is especially important if one spouse has complained that the other can't be affectionate without being sexual.)

Set a loving mood early in the day. Give "Good morning" and "Good night" kisses whenever possible. Show tenderness. Smile warmly at your spouse. Cuddle in bed a few extra minutes. Don't leave in the morning without a kiss or hug. Ask if there is something you can do that would make your partner's day go a little easier. Call during the day to say "Hi." If you had an argument the night before, don't spend the morning sulking or complaining. If the argument can't be settled before work, say you'll settle it that night and do your best to be pleasant. (You can be angry with each other and still be pleasant.)

Once in a while, schedule lovemaking at least twelve hours ahead of time. That gives each of you time to gear up, fantasize about it, and accomplish all the minor tasks that might ordinarily intrude on your time together. A nice touch: call your mate or leave a short note expressing some sexual fantasy you have about the upcoming event.

For your next two lovemaking sessions, plan not to reach orgasm. Neither of you. You can come close to orgasm if you'd like, but stop short of that final pleasure. Without that common goal in mind, you and your mate will have lingering foreplay and sensual body caresses. You'll delight in sensations you ordinarily ignore. You'll likely learn something new about what pleases your partner. And when you finally do reach orgasm later, you'll enjoy it all the more.

To improve desire, think of a time when you were head-over-heels attracted to your mate. Visualize the scene fully. What essential qualities from that scene does your mate still possess? A certain look, a smile, a way of speaking, a way of touching? Sometimes, a little preparation (by way of fantasy) can improve your desire for, and enjoyment of, sex.

Did You Know . . .

. . . that one of the most reliable ways to measure and monitor your marital happiness is the following (assuming good physical health): Calculate the number of times you had intercourse in a certain time frame (say, two weeks) and subtract the number of arguments you had. (An argument occurred any time one spouse became "uncooperative"). If the answer is a positive number, you're probably happy. If it's a negative number, you're probably not.*

This method *reflects* marital happiness. It is not a formula for improving happiness, per se. Automatically increasing the frequency of intercourse or reducing the number of arguments won't necessarily make you a happy couple. But it is a good way to monitor your progress in improving the happiness in your marriage.

* Howard, John W. and Dawes, Robyn M. Linear prediction of marital happiness. *Personality and Social Psychology Bulletin*, 1976, 2, 478-480

If sex has become a bit stale and predictable, agree with your mate to have more spontaneous sex about once a week. (By definition, spontaneous sex is unplanned and occurs at a time or place not usually set aside for making love.) Take turns initiating it. When your mate is the initiator, then you have the privilege of deciding where, how, and how long you'll make love together.

To increase intimacy (and possibly sexual desire) read a novel to your partner. It helps make an isolated act (reading) an intimate one, and can add to your excitement if there are any erotic passages in the book.

To improve desire, write a love letter to your mate from an unpredictable point of view. Write things you've thought but ordinarily would not say. Imagine, for instance, the reasons another person might lust after your spouse and write a letter from the perspective of that imaginary person.[9]

This exercise helps you to loosen up rigid perceptions, remove blind spots, and heighten your arousal in a mate you sometimes take for granted.

Care about your appearance and your health. Very few of us have the shape and stamina of Olympic athletes, but all of us can try to look and dress in a manner that appeals to our mate. Plump or scrawny, the right outfit, cologne, or hairstyle can really please a partner. And there is nothing like knowing you are attractive to your mate to make you feel good about yourself and more sexually alive.

Keep in Mind

- Sincere, open revelation of feelings is the most intimate thing you can do. Wives really are stimulated by it and husbands need to discover it isn't fatal.

- There is a tendency for men in their middle-adult years to be more sensual (as opposed to genital) in their sexual approach.

- It's okay not to feel like having sex, but never withhold sex as a punishment.

- There will be occasions when sex is less exciting or absent altogether. If your partner is going through a sexually quiet period, making demands won't help. Remain physically affectionate and emotionally in touch with your partner, and neither you nor your mate will feel rejected or misunderstood.[10]

Secret #24

Keeping It Between the Two of You

When the tension between two people rises to an uncomfortable level, an interesting phenomenon often occurs: a third person gets drawn into the scene to distract the twosome from their conflict. That lowers their anxiety but postpones any opportunity for the two to resolve their conflict by themselves. Sometimes the third person gets pulled into the two-person system (as when a wife, frustrated with her husband, calls her mother to complain). Sometimes the third person enters voluntarily in order to rescue one of the two, serve as a referee to both, or simply divert attention away from the quarreling duo (as when a young child spills her milk and distracts her arguing parents, or a father intervenes between a quarreling mother and son). When a duo becomes a trio in the manner just described, an *emotional triangle* has formed.[1]

Emotional triangles are everywhere. (Ever been to a party where many of the people don't know one another? Often they lower their anxiety by diverting their attention to something safe, like a beverage or a television program. "Excuse me, I need a refill . . .") Being in a triangle is not a problem. But remaining in a triangle, is. Why? Because when a triangle forms, the basic problems between two people don't get resolved. They get reshelved—put on hold. A reshelved problem lowers anxiety in the short run but adds anxiety in the long run, as problems and issues accumulate like unopened bills. Examples:

- The wife who chronically complains to her (supportive) mother about her husband comes away more convinced that her spouse is a louse and resists looking at her role in the marital problem. Consequently, the marriage remains troubled and the woman continues to complain to her mom about it.

- The husband who routinely intervenes when his wife and son argue prevents them from solving their own problems. Mother and son may even get to the point where they rely on dad to intervene. When that happens, dad usually walks away from the situation with more anxiety than the other two, and he risks alienating his wife or son, who may believe he's taking sides unfairly.

- The child who routinely distracts his parents from fighting by complaining of physical aches or by causing trouble risks becoming the family scapegoat. Mom and Dad may never fully resolve their marital problems, because when things get heated between them, they can count on their child or the child's problems to divert them.

Sometimes the third point in the emotional triangle is not a person. As Kyle became more unhappy with Karen, he found ways to spend more time working; his job was the third point. Karen then had a new issue to complain about, and Kyle tried to spend even *more* time away from home.

Clues to Hidden Triangles

Triangles operate freely because participants rarely know they are in them. Problematic children who interrupt quarreling parents don't make a conscious decision to intrude, and the quarreling parents don't make a conscious decision to argue within earshot of the over-involved child. Many people caught in the middle between two others have noble intentions. They wish to ease another person's pain or help heal the troubled relationship. But on a subconscious level it is their own pain (the need to feel loved, competent, or in control) that drives them.

How can you tell whether you are trapped in an emotional triangle? The more common clues are:

- Finding yourself "in the middle" of a conflict between two other people. (Or always seeking out a third person to help you lower your anxiety in your relationship with someone else.)

- Feeling responsible for solving other people's problems.

- Gossip (talking about a third person behind his back).

- The presence of a scapegoat or "black sheep." (As long as there is someone else to blame for your misery, you never have to face yourself.)

- Arguments or conflicts that never get resolved.

- Being emotionally cut off from a member of your family. (If a man cuts himself off from his relationship with "toxic parents," his expectations of his wife will be higher. Should she not meet his expectations, he'll likely cut himself off from her, too. Emotional cut-offs are fine for a while but are poor long-term solutions.)

Disconnecting yourself from an emotional triangle isn't easy. Since the purpose of a triangle is to reduce anxiety, disconnecting yourself will serve to *raise* anxiety temporarily. Consequently you'll be strongly tempted to rejoin the triangle and stabilize the situation.

Marge used to listen (unhappily) for hours while her mother complained to her about her "selfish and lazy" father. (Marge was the last child to leave home and felt guilty for doing so.) Finally she told her mother, "I feel bad that you are so unhappy. But from now on I think you should talk to Dad directly or perhaps see a counselor." Her mom acted hurt and angry, which made Marge feel guilty. She almost agreed to listen to her mom's complaints but was able to stand her ground ("Mom, I'm going to hang up now.") That made her mom more angry. Her mom didn't call back for two weeks. Instead she called Marge's brother and complained to him about Marge (another triangle). Fortunately, the brother was a psychologist who knew all about emotional triangles. He knew it would be a mistake to agree with his mom that Marge was wrong, or to try to talk to Marge on his mom's behalf. Instead, he simply acknowledged to his mom that she seemed upset and wished her good luck in resolving her problem. That frustrated Mom but kept most of the anxiety where it should have been—between Mom and her husband, not in the laps of Marge or her brother.

Happy couples deal with each other directly. If they call on a third person for advice (such as a counselor or friend), they do not try to get that person to be a judge or jury, they do not betray their spouse by making biased accusations behind his or her back, and they realize that the problems will ultimately be resolved only between the two of them through constructive dialogue.

Are you trapped in an emotional triangle?

What to Do

Identify the triangles in which you participate; otherwise, you can't unhook yourself. In which relationships are you the "middleman?" Do you gossip or do others gossip to you, resulting in further alienation between you and someone else? When tension is high between you and another, how does that tension diminish? Does one of you get distracted by a third person? ("It's time to put the kids to bed . . .") or an event? ("We can't talk now, it's time to go to bed.") Detecting triangles requires you to be a bit detached from the ordinary push and pull of a situation. If it's too difficult noticing your own triangles, begin by hunting for triangles that don't involve you. For example, have you overheard two co-workers complaining about a third? Watch your favorite television program (soap operas and situation comedies about families are perfect) and search for triangles there. Once you've identified a few, you may be more adept at identifying triangles of your own making.

To unhook yourself from a triangle where you are caught in the middle, use reflective listening (see page 23) and don't offer advice. Unhooking yourself is a delicate operation. You must detach yourself from the emotional pressure to get involved but still remain connected to the other people. (Running and hiding doesn't remove you from a triangle. It's your emotional involvement more than your physical presence that is required to keep a triangle in operation.) Summarizing what the other person just said to you—"So you're telling me that you're lonely living with Dad"—is a way of staying connected without getting caught up in the problem.

Repeat yourself. If caught in the middle and reflective listening doesn't bring relief, be a broken record. Tell the complaining person to talk directly to the one being complained about, not to you. Say it over and over. If that doesn't help, you can exit the situation (by leaving or hanging up) but *do not leave in anger or frustration.* Better to say, "I know you're frustrated by your problem but I don't like being in the middle. I'm going to hang up now but I'll talk to you soon. Good luck." Remember, as long as you are emotionally charged, you can't unhook yourself from a triangle.

Do it on purpose. Once you and your partner agree that triangles are a problem for you, purposely "triangle in" a third person during discussions with your spouse—then attempt to disconnect the triangle. Sometimes the best way to reduce behavior patterns that are automatic is to force yourself to do it more frequently. Doing so makes you much more aware of a process that ordinarily occurs automatically. Once that happens, you can change that process more easily than if you weren't aware.

Did You Know . . .

. . . that health problems, rather than a person, can be the third point in an emotional triangle? When that happens, relationship problems persist, but so do the health problems (since they are needed to stabilize an unstable relationship). A common example might be developing a headache so you don't have to attend a family reunion. But more subtle examples exist, too.

Joan Atwood, coordinator of marriage and family counseling at Hofstra University, wrote about the role of premenstrual mood changes on a couple's relationship.* Of the 100 women interviewed, 68 said they felt sad or depressed prior to their period, 32 felt anxious, and 19 felt angry or edgy. Forty-five reported that their mood changes affected their interpersonal relationships. Atwood indicated that the mood changes can sometimes be the third leg in an emotional triangle. For example, a husband might dismiss his wife's legitimate marital complaints as "only due to PMS." Or, some women who ordinarily keep their feelings in check might allow themselves to express pent-up anger without guilt. ("After all, it's not me, it's my PMS that's talking.") PMS, like any chronic physical condition, may enable people to avoid dealing with relevant issues in a direct, constructive way.

*Atwood, Joan. Effects of premenstrual mood changes in the couple's relationship. *The Family Psychologist*, 7(3), 1991, p. 17-19.

Once you've successfully unhooked yourself from a triangle, answer this question: What would have to happen for you to get re-involved in the same triangle? Once out of a triangle, there will be great pressure for you to return. Predicting ahead of time what the pressure will be and how you might resist it will improve the odds that you can stay out of problematic triangles. *Hint:* one useful way of resisting pressure is to inform the other person (before he tries to re-involve you in the triangle) what he'll probably say or do to try to re-involve you. Such a prediction reduces the other person's influence over you.

Keep in Mind

- Middlemen never receive the appreciation they feel they deserve and usually end up with most of the anxiety.

- If you must talk with someone else about your marital problem, commit to talking with your mate about the issue at least twice as long as you discuss it with someone else.

- If you must talk with someone else about your marital problem, tell your spouse everything you told to the third person and tell the third person that everything being discussed will be told to your spouse. No exceptions.

- If you are in the middle, the only piece of advice you should offer is this: "Don't talk to me about your problem. Talk to the person with whom you're having the problem."

Secret #25

Spiritual Beliefs and Shared Values

It's one of those statistics that catches your eye and makes you say "No, that can't be!" But according to a ground-breaking Gallup survey, happiness in a marriage is better predicted by how often a couple prays together than by how often they make love.[1] And there's more. Couples who pray together (compared to couples who don't) report having greater respect for their mate (83 percent versus 62 percent), agree on how to raise children (73 percent versus 59 percent), are more playful (56 percent versus 45 percent), and believe their mate is a skilled lover (62 percent versus 49 percent). Individual prayer correlates with marital happiness, too, but joint prayer correlates at a level twice as high.

For couples where at least one partner seriously considered divorce but who since have reconciled, 85 percent engaged in joint prayer. While other factors were also associated with reconciliation (such as equality, ability to disagree constructively, and frequency of sex), none made the impact that joint prayer apparently made.

Religion and spirituality play a more important role in marital happiness than most people realize. In the Gallup survey, religious beliefs enhanced marital stability for people of all ages (not just for older folk, who tend to be more religious and maritally secure). A fluke?

According to a 1990 university study,[2] *decades* of research have demonstrated that people highly involved in religion have the happiest marriages. But those findings have been ignored by social scientists, according to the authors.

How does religion contribute to marital satisfaction? No one knows for sure. Some point to the fact that religion helps people make sense of their lives. It provides meaning. People who lack meaning are less happy, not only in their marriages but in virtually every aspect of their lives (family, career, friendships, etc.).[3,4] But religion is also about a sense of values. While a person can certainly be virtuous without being religious, religion emphasizes those qualities most of us would consider virtuous: honesty, integrity, responsibility, commitment, forgiveness, and compassion. In one study, "virtuous" men and women were found to be happily married and fulfilled parents. They had better health. They were "cheerful, optimistic, hopeful, decisive, energetic, . . . reliable . . . tender, open, and loyal."[5]

Inter-Faith Marriage: A Blessing?

You increase the odds of having a successful marriage if you and your mate are of the same religious faith.[6] Inter-faith couples do have a slightly higher divorce rate than same-faith couples. On measures of happiness, same-faith couples are happier than inter-faith couples, who are happier than couples where one or both partners have no religious faith. Sociologist Norval Glenn believes that inter-faith marriages, or marriages where one partner is non-religious, become stressed when the decision must be made as to what the religious education of the children will be. The parent whose beliefs are not formally taught to the children often feels more on the periphery of the family, especially if unique religious rituals are followed. Nevertheless, many inter-faith couples succeed in their marriages; they may just require more tolerance and understanding.

The Grace Scale

Sociologist and priest Andrew Greeley hypothesized that the warmer and more passionate one's religious images, the warmer and more passionate one's marriage, and vice versa. He asked people to select one descriptor from each of the following four pairs regarding their image of God: was God a

> Mother or Father?
>
> Master or Spouse?
>
> Judge or Lover?
>
> Friend or King?

The more "warm" one's image of God (God as Mother, Spouse, Lover, and Friend), the higher one's score on the "grace scale." Statistically, those scoring highest on the grace scale were generally twice as likely than those scoring lowest to report satisfying and intense sexual relationships with their mate.[7] Fulfilling, uninhibited physical intimacy correlated strongly with warmer images of God.

Greeley's conclusion: "The couple that plays and prays together stays together—and has a rich and rewarding sexual life, especially if their intimacy correlates with warm images of God."[8]

Does your marriage need a spiritual lift?

What to Do

Go to church more often. For many of us, churchgoing is a once-in-a-

---

Did You Know . . .

. . . that evidence of the power of prayer exists in scientific literature, and that some evidence is nothing short of astounding? In his book *Recovering The Soul*, physician Larry Dossey described numerous experiments where some batches of germinating seeds were prayed for, and other batches were not.* Was there a difference in the rate of germination? Amazingly, prayed-for seeds grew more shoots than non-prayed-for seeds (in a study repeated many times). Experimenters then "stressed" some seeds by adding salt water to the seed container. Numerous repetitions of the experiment were conducted, with greater amounts of salt being added each time. Results were consistent and striking: prayer worked even better when the seeds were under stress. Finally, researchers were interested in answering this question: which type of prayer, directed or non-directed, works best? (Directed prayer occurs when the person prays for a specific outcome. Non-directed prayer occurs when the person prays for "whatever is best"—what researchers called a "thy will be done" approach.) Results were unequivocal and fascinating: while both types of prayer worked, non-directed prayer brought results almost twice as powerful as directed prayer.

While these studies were not about marriage, the findings might bring encouragement to those of you who use prayer to influence your marriage.

* Dossey, Larry. *Recovering the Soul.* New York: Bantam, 1989, p.54-62.

while ritual at best. If you've been thinking about returning to church (or attending more frequently) why not try it for a few months? If you have children, discuss with them why you're changing your churchgoing habits and the value of church attendance. To improve motivation, attend a service that other friends will be attending. Get together for coffee or breakfast afterward.

Select some personal virtue you'd like to enhance and make a pact with yourself to improve upon it for the next several weeks. (Since nobody is perfect, improvement is possible.) Perhaps you wish to show more honesty, compassion, tolerance, gratitude, or kindness. Daily self-reminders can keep you on track. If you'd prefer, make it a family project. Young children can learn more about virtuous behavior and in the process the family unit can be strengthened.

If you have an inter-faith marriage, don't allow differences in dogma to diminish caring, intimacy, and family involvement. You can participate in some of your spouses's religious rituals—if appropriate to the ceremony—without renouncing your own beliefs. (Or, if you prefer, you can participate in the preparation for those rituals—baking certain foods, purchasing gifts, etc.). You can ask your children questions about their religious education classes without challenging what they've been taught. You can express your differing views to the children in a manner that shows acceptance of what they've been taught. Religious differences don't have to make a difference.

Keep in Mind

- Religion becomes a more important force in life the older you become.

- Research findings suggest that adding a dose of religion or prayer to your daily routine won't hurt and may help.

- Religion may not improve happiness or fairness in your life, but it can make your life more meaningful.

Secret #26

Holding Hands During Adversity

If you live long enough and love hard enough, loss and pain is inevitable. Health problems, financial setbacks, relationship strains, the death of a loved one or the death of a dream, eventually find their way to the doorsteps of the happiest couples. Next year,

- Over eight hundred thousand people will be told, "You have cancer."

- Over forty million people will be admitted to a hospital.

- Birth defects or stillbirths will account for 3 percent of all births.

- About one million couples will divorce. Many more will remain in difficult, unsatisfying marriages.

Coping with adversity isn't easy. Especially if the hard times are chronic (coping with a permanent injury or the death of a loved one), mobilizing your resources over an extended period of time can be exhausting. But when partners can count on each other for support, the tough times can be made more bearable.

Are You a Confident Confidante?

When anxiety rises during a crisis, coping efforts become more rigid. Someone who likes the company of others during minor difficulties may demand *togetherness* during moments of intense stress. Alternatively, someone who prefers time alone when stressed may go into hiding when matters seem overwhelming. All the skills that couples use to keep their marriage healthy during calm times—negotiation, compromise, tolerance, understanding—are stretched to the limit during a crisis. Pete and Patty went through hard times when he lost his job. Some days, when no job interviews were scheduled and Pete returned home from the unemployment office feeling forlorn, he just wanted to be left alone.

"How did it go?" Patty would ask.

"The same."

"Well, you should hear back from some of the other companies this week. I'm sure they were impressed with your application."

"Yeah, sure," he'd mumble, walking out of the room.

"I just wanted to know how he was doing," Pat confided to me later. "I wanted him to know I was there for him, that I don't consider him a failure, and that together we'll get through this. Why won't he let me help him?"

Many men have a harder time asking for help than do women. Sometimes they don't want to appear weak, or they don't want to add to their spouse's burdens, so they retreat into themselves. For a short-term problem, such a withdrawal probably won't have adverse effects and may help the situation if the man is able to sort things out for himself. But when problems drag on, retreating may add to the difficulties as partners feel more and more disconnected from each other.

Sometimes, being a confidante to one's mate requires putting aside your own needs temporarily so as to meet the needs of the partner. In the above example, Patty's frustration was not just because Pete wanted to be left alone. She was frustrated because she wanted to engage him in conversation. She believed it was in his best interests to talk (and she was right) and she felt less competent as a spouse when he didn't respond the way she wanted. A more helpful way for Patty to respond might have been, "It looks like you'd rather be alone for a while. Why don't I call you when dinner's ready? I do want to talk to you about some things, but I'm willing to wait until later."

During trying times, couples often unwittingly "take turns" coping well. As such, one is always available to the other. Most of us still have to go to work, take care of the children, and tend to the business of everyday life despite some personal crisis. Knowing that a spouse can "take over" and provide you with a temporary respite can be enough to help you through the worst of times.

The Plus Side of Adversity

Think for a moment of all the different friends you've had over your lifetime. Chances are, the friends you still feel closest to—even if you live a thousand miles away and rarely see one another—are the ones who were by your side during some challenging time of your life. Trying times have a way of bonding relationships. If a couple can get through hard times with no blaming and a greater sense of connectedness, a special bond develops that time cannot weaken. Knowing that you survived a personal or family crisis can also increase your confidence in being able to cope with future adversity.

Adversity also helps to make your life more meaningful. As often as not, trying times help you to reprioritize your values. You learn to appreciate the importance of your relationships. Little things you'd ordinarily overlook become precious in your eyes.

It's possible, and necessary, to hold hands with your mate during difficult times. Each of you may have your idiosyncratic ways of coping, but staying connected to your mate can be a soothing balm in an otherwise painful period.

What to Do

If your mate is troubled by a loss or other painful situation, give her first the message "I love you," not the message "You need me." A sense of control is important in coping. Taking complete charge or giving advice prematurely without getting a clear sense of what your mate really needs may diminish her sense of control.

Accept, never challenge, a grieving partner's feelings. Don't try to talk him out of feelings just because they make you uncomfortable or you don't understand them. A spouse who feels misunderstood may turn away from you at a time when your presence can be beneficial. Listen fully and summarize what your partner tells you so that each of you can be sure it was fully understood.

Take turns. If you and your mate have opposite ways of coping—he wants time alone, you want time together; you want to be able to talk on a moment's notice, he prefers scheduled dialogues, etc.—agree to take turns having things handled your way. For example, on odd days of the month your spouse gets his way. On even days, you get your way.[1] Knowing in advance that your needs won't get swept aside helps build patience and tolerance of your partner's needs.

Encourage, but don't insist, that your mate "talk out" his troubling feelings. Some people aren't comfortable expressing difficult feelings. While it is more healthy for them to talk, persistent efforts to get them to talk may backfire. Some men feel they must be "the strong one" in the family. To discuss painful feelings can make them feel weak. Others fear that expressing deep feelings will cause them to lose emotional control. Some ways to help encourage a reluctant spouse to express him- or herself:

- Suggest that she write out her feelings (privately).

- Ask him to help you understand why he prefers not to discuss his feelings. Tell him you won't debate or challenge his reasons why, but that you would like to better understand.

- Speculate what you think she may be feeling. Example: "It wouldn't surprise me if you felt scared . . ."

- Comment that he must be feeling lonely.

- When feelings are expressed, never challenge them or try to talk the person out of them. She will feel misunderstood and may stop talking. Better to use reflective listening (see page 23).

- Request a regularly scheduled, time-limited discussion. That way, you get the dialogue you need, and your partner can take comfort knowing that the rest of the time he or she won't be challenged to talk.

Don't hold your feelings back to "protect" your mate. You don't have to accuse or be critical, but it's important to admit when you are scared or angry. Holding back feelings will add to your stress and may not relieve your spouse of any. (A mate may be worried about you if he or she detects that you are not being honest about your feelings). Suppressing feelings adds emotional distance between the two of you at a time when you need to be a working team.

Reassure the children. During stressful times, young children worry, too. That may show up as temper tantrums, disobedience, school or social problems, or withdrawal. If there is something they can *reasonably* do that will ease your burdens (a few more chores, making fewer requests for new clothes or extra spending money, etc.), ask for their help and show your appreciation. Most important, spend extra quality time with them. "Nothing will convince them better that Mom and Dad are coping than having fun as a family. Just because Mom and Dad are worried adults doesn't mean they have to be unhappy parents."[2]

When the crisis has passed (or there is a lull), take some time for the two of you to be alone together. Go away for a weekend trip. Hire a sitter for the kids and spend the day relaxing with your mate. Especially after a prolonged crisis, it might take a little time for the two of you to feel completely at ease. Have patience, show consideration, and make your relationship the number-one priority.

Keep in Mind

● Being a burden to a spouse is not always a burden. Especially for short-lived problems, most spouses are equipped to be

---

Did You Know . . .

. . . that men and women often have different approaches to grief? In a study of 127 parents whose child died from Sudden Infant Death Syndrome, 85 percent of the partners did not match each other in their grief response.* Most men cried less, talked less often about the death, and expressed less emotion than their wives. Yet according to the researchers, the men suffered as much as the women. (They were better at hiding their suffering, however. Fathers felt a responsibility to be caretaker and a source of strength for their wives.) Both parents faced the dilemma of having to grieve their loss and at the same time deal with their day-to-day responsibilities. The other children still needed attention, and somebody had to return to work sooner than desired in order to provide for the family.

Still, the couples in the study did an excellent job in helping each other cope with the loss. Those who coped best did not fall prey to strict social stereotypes. The mothers were not always over-emotional and helpless, the husbands were not always strong and silent. Each grieved, and each allowed the other to grieve without blaming, chastising, or making unreasonable demands.

*DeFrain, John Learning about grief from normal families: SIDS, stillbirth, and miscarriage. *Journal of Marriage and Family Therapy*, *17*(3), 1991, 215-232.

"the strong one" for a while. Besides, partners want to make sacrifices for one another from time to time.

- All problems are temporary. They either disappear or we somehow manage to adjust to them and move forward. Even if the pain doesn't completely go away, it doesn't have to get in your way.

- Problems don't make or break you. It's your response to a problem that is vital to your success.

- In trying times, your spouse is coping in the way he or she thinks is for the best. Keep that in mind if you want your mate to do something different.

Secret #27

Knowing How (and When) to Forgive

To genuinely forgive after suffering a deep hurt or loss is one of the hardest things you will ever do.

Some people forgive quickly, not out of sincere love and understanding but out of fear. Motivated to avoid rejection, to gain approval, or to appease, they "forgive" for the wrong reasons and never feel completely free.

Some withhold forgiveness until they "get to the bottom" of what happened. Betrayed spouses often ask question after endless question in an attempt to discover the "truth": (*Does he really love me? Would he ever betray me again? What was his real reason for betraying me?*) Never knowing for sure when they've discovered the truth, they can't free themselves to forgive.

Some confuse forgiveness with forgetting. Forgetting is not a sign of forgiveness. The deeper the hurt, the longer you will remember it. But when you forgive and feel free to resume trusting, more of your time is spent doing positive things and your mind is no longer preoccupied with the hurt.

Some withhold forgiveness, not merely out of vengeance but as a way to exercise control over a relationship that got out of control. "I was made a fool. I'll be damned if I let her hurt me that way again." An understandable sentiment but one that, if maintained, becomes self-defeating.

The challenges of forgiveness are many. Listen to Marian.

"I've tried to forgive, I really have. But each day when I wake up the feeling isn't there. How can I forgive him when I don't *feel* forgiving?"

A common mistake made by well-intentioned people is to believe they must feel forgiving before they can finally forgive. While it is not helpful to pretend you are no longer hurt and angry when you are, forgiveness begins as a decision, not as a feeling. You must first choose to forgive before you can ever feel forgiving.

Forgiveness is also a challenge because there is a tendency to quickly forget what was right about a relationship after we have been wronged. One woman, after she learned that her husband had had a brief affair two years earlier, totally revised her view of him. "I couldn't help myself," she explained. "I'd remember all the times he went out of his way to do something nice for me. I used to think he was wonderful for doing those things. Now I think he did it to trick me, to keep me off his trail. Maybe he was considerate because he felt guilty, I'm not sure. All I know is that I'm questioning everything he did for me. Everything." In fact, her relationship had brought her years of joy—all of which, sadly, had become suspect.

"I'm Sorry, But . . ."

It's amazing how many partners never apologize for their hurtful actions. Sometimes they blame their behavior on their spouse, claiming "You made me do it." Sometimes they do apologize ". . . but you must understand that I was under a lot of pressure at the time . . ." Saying "I'm sorry, but . . ." rarely feels like a sincere apology. These half-hearted apologies are understandable, however. Often, the person is trying to *explain* his or her actions, but the explanation is misinterpreted as an attempt to *justify* the actions. Sometimes the betrayed person unwittingly puts the explaining spouse in a double bind.

"Why did you hurt me like that?"

"I don't know."

"You don't know? How can I ever learn to trust you if you say you don't know. Surely you must know something?"

"Maybe I hurt you because I was angry at you for being so controlling and demanding. I'm not your possession."

"Oh, so you're telling me it's my fault you flirted with your boss?"

In this case, the husband's attempt to know why his wife acted flirtatiously prompted her to give an explanation that sounded self-serving. But having no explanation was not acceptable to him, either.

Bringing Up the Past

Efforts to forgive get sidetracked when one partner focuses on past injustices while the other wants to focus only on the current problems. While most self-help books advise against re-washing old laundry, diversions to the past usually happen for good reasons. Rather than make a blanket-rule disallowing any excursions into the past, it is best to inquire (sincerely, not sarcastically) why it is important for a spouse to bring up old issues. (For example, when you believe your mate is downplaying his offense, you may be bringing up past issues as a way to impress upon your partner the extent of your pain.) Simply accusing—"Why must you keep bringing up *that* old issue?"—may add insult to injury and further complicate the forgiveness process. If the issue of bringing up the past continues to sidetrack your efforts at forgiveness, take turns having discussions where the past is allowed and disallowed as a topic.

Phases of Forgiveness

In the book *The Forgiving Marriage*,[1] five phases of forgiveness were outlined. Not everyone needs to go through each phase in order to experience forgiveness, and some people must repeat certain phases, but for the most part they represent the typical steps taken in forgiveness and reconciliation.

Phase One.

Identify the hurt. Distorting the truth complicates forgiveness. If you pretend you weren't really hurt when in fact you were, you won't see the need to forgive. But you will harbor anxiety and never feel fully content with the relationship. If you can acknowledge the hurt, you must then examine it more closely. Were you hurt like that before? By whom? How did you handle it then? At Phase One, the hurtful person needs to own up to being hurtful and examine what caused it.

Phase Two.

Confess, if guilty, or confront, if betrayed. Say "I'm sorry" and mean it. Try to explain your understanding of why you did what you did, but don't make excuses. Failure to accept responsibility for your actions will impede reconciliation.

If you've been hurt, say so. Sometimes forgiveness is possible without letting the person know how he hurt you, but reconciliation will be stifled without an honest confrontation. Holding back feelings can leave a relationship scarred, just as much as hurting your partner can. Try not to attack or demean your mate. Be direct. Confrontation helps you let go of the hurt and communicates trust and a desire for growth.

Phase Three.

Have a dialogue with your partner for the purpose of gaining understanding. Reflective listening is a useful tool here (see page 23). The dialogue should not be an inquisition. No one should be an interrogator ready to pass judgment. The goal is to discover what led up to the hurtful actions. Even if you were the one betrayed, examining your role in the relationship is vital at this phase. You did not "cause" your partner's infidelity, but you may have been contributing to the unhappiness in the marriage. Remember, the dialogue to understanding is necessarily limited. It is difficult to ascertain all the reasons why things happened the way they did.

Phase Four.

Forgive, and make reparation if at all possible. If you've identified the hurts; if you've confessed and expressed remorse for pain you've caused; if you've confronted the person who hurt you and have discussed the fears and concerns you each have; if you've come up with some plan of action to lessen the possibility of future hurt; if you wish to be reconciled; then you are ready to forgive. Forgiveness is not an effortless next step but an awkward leap. It is risking being hurt again in order to grow in a relationship that is important to you.

Phase Five.

Let go of lingering resentments and guilt. Remnant feelings of anger and guilt may arise from time to time. That does not necessarily mean you haven't been fully forgiving. Reminding yourself of the good aspects of both your mate and of your relationship can help steer you away from pain and toward contentment. Sometimes what you must let go of are longstanding myths. Maybe you believed your mate would be all-perfect. Maybe you believed that love meant never having to say you're sorry. Regardless, leaving behind what you have outgrown is required of a healthy, satisfying life.

If you have ever forgiven someone, or been forgiven, then you know how possible true forgiveness is. But it does require effort, patience, and commitment. When you wish to forgive (yourself or someone else), some additional guidelines can help.

What to Do

Allow an unimpeded opportunity to express pain. For three days during the week (more or less, if needed) set aside ten to twenty minutes to recite your list of grievances. Your partner is to listen, summarizing so as to convey he heard you, but not to challenge or debate you. After the third day your partner is to write a letter of apology for the hurts against you and for his role in the weakening of the marriage. He should admit guilt when he is guilty and ask for forgiveness. Then do the exercise again, this time reversing roles.

As uncomfortable as this might be, it allows you to clear the air and express yourself in an unimpeded manner. And it provides the opportunity for a well-thought-out apology.

Act forgiving, even if you don't feel forgiving. How would you be acting today (or during the next hour) if you had forgiven your mate? Act accordingly. You are not denying your pain in this exercise but helping to move past your anger and toward reconciliation. If you wait to feel forgiving before you act forgiving, you may have to wait a much longer time than you deserve.

Do the "I forgive you" task.[2] Imagine the other person is seated directly across from you. Repeat aloud the words *I forgive you* and notice the thoughts that follow. Did you think "But I'm still angry" or "You don't deserve forgiveness"? Repeat the phrase *I forgive you* and again notice your thoughts. Doing this about ten times results in one of two outcomes: either no thoughts follow the phrase and you simply feel more forgiving, or one thought continues to recur. In the latter case, the recurring thought represents some unresolved issue for you. Recognizing that allows you the opportunity to examine that issue closely or talk it over with your mate. The "I forgive you" exercise helps you either way.

If you've been forgiven but your mate still mentions the hurt against her, don't criticize. Resentment and anger doesn't vanish immediately after forgiveness, despite best intentions. And some places or situations—a certain restaurant, day of the week, etc.—may remind your mate of what you did that was hurtful. Understand that she still needs to talk about it from time to time, and understand that her mood may fluctuate. Don't take it personally and don't condemn her for her feelings. Say instead, "I don't blame you for having those feelings. I wish you didn't have to feel that way, but I understand it's not easy to forget." That demonstrates compassion and understanding and probably will hasten her recovery.

Pray. Pray for the ability to be forgiving, and pray for your spouse who has hurt you. Seeking help from a higher power makes a difference to many people. And praying for the person who hurt you helps nurture compassion, a necessary quality of a forgiving heart.

Perform a ritual together to symbolize your renewal in your marriage. Plant a tree or garden in honor of your future together. Renew your marriage vows. Buy a wedding cake. Give your partner a small gift or piece of jewelry—something to symbolize your reconciliation and love for one another. Such a ritual helps put emotional closure on some bad feelings and is a nice way to begin a new future together.

Keep in Mind

- "I forgive you" is as important a phrase as "I love you."

- If you still feel resentful, you feel owed. What are you owed? If you still feel guilty, you feel you owe. What do you owe?

- Forgiveness begins as a decision, not a feeling.

- Apologies can soothe but they do not heal. Apologies should be sincere, not said in an offhand way.

- Whoever hurt you did so not because you were unlovable but because he or she had weaknesses.

Secret #28

Being Positively Optimistic

You don't need a major, upsetting calamity in your life to become depressed. In one study, daily hassles (minor arguments, broken machinery, traffic tie-ups, etc.) predicted depression better than did major life events (serious illness, death of loved one, etc.).[1] And if your marriage is not satisfying, chances are that the ordinary day-to-day hassles will be even more upsetting. Why? Because unhappy, pessimistic thoughts breed more unhappy thoughts. When you are happy and all is well in your life, a fender-bender or an insensitive remark from your spouse can be shrugged off. But when you are unhappy, such events make you feel frustrated, less in charge of your life, which can cultivate a "Why is everyone against me?" attitude. Pessimism has a way of clouding over all aspects of your life, not just the troubling parts. Men and women in unhappy marriages can become pessimistic. That is one reason why they are twenty-five times more likely to be depressed than couples in a satisfying marriage.

You Gotta Have Hope!

"Hope is essential to human endeavor, and successful couples have it."[2] Optimists are healthier and happier and live longer than pessimists. They are more creative, better problem solvers, and more friendly and helpful. When adversity strikes, optimists are more likely to persevere, to accept life's challenges, to cope well, and to collect fewer scars. Not pessimists. Pessimists are likely to give up sooner, especially when the going gets tough. And pessimists are more likely to become depressed during trying times. Compare the following pessimistic/optimistic comments. See for yourself how one's attitude can generate either happiness or misery.

OPTIMISTIC: "Even if we disagree, I know my wife will eventually understand how I feel, and I'll understand her."

PESSIMISTIC: "My wife never understands me."

OPTIMISTIC: "This hasn't been an easy time for us but we're confident we'll get through it. We'll find a way."

PESSIMISTIC: "We've tried to work things out. Nothing helps."

OPTIMISTIC: "We'll just keep trying until we succeed."

PESSIMISTIC: "Things improved for a while until my husband went back to his old ways. Why bother trying again?"

Each of the "optimistic" examples reflects one of the three underpinnings to hope. First, hope takes root when you feel *understood*. Knowing that your thoughts and feelings make sense—that you are not crazy or foolish—gives you reason to believe that answers to your concerns exist and may be forthcoming. Believing that your spouse (especially) understands you (versus his insisting you "shouldn't feel that way") enhances togetherness and can protect you from despair. Unhappy couples often feel misunderstood by their mates, which diminishes their hope that they can resolve differences.

Second, hope is nourished when you possess *faith*—not merely a blind faith that matters will work out—but a faith that resources are available to you to make success likely. When you have friends and family who care, your outlook isn't quite so bleak. And when you believe you possess the skills necessary to get you through a difficult period, it's easier to feel optimistic. Most unhappy couples don't believe they possess adequate problem-solving or communication skills, and consequently feel more hopeless.

Finally, hope requires *committed work*. The hopeful persevere despite setbacks. Unhappy couples, feeling weary, misunderstood, and short on faith, abandon efforts to improve the relationship much sooner.

No matter what your difficulty, if you can trust that someone *understands* your pain; if you can nurture the *faith* that you have the resources to cope; and if you *commit* yourself to overcoming your difficulties; hope will thrive, and so will you.

Overcoming Pessimism: The Three P's

Dr. Martin Seligman at the University of Pennsylvania is perhaps the world's leading authority on optimism. He wondered what rationale people used to explain why bad things (or good things) happened to them. A person's "explanatory style" accounted for his or her optimism or pessimism. Seligman noted three crucial dimensions to one's explanatory style: did one take it *personally*? And were the effects *permanent* and *pervasive*?[3] In hard times, pessimists blamed themselves unrealistically (took it too personally), believed the difficulties would go on a long time (permanent), and saw the negativity affecting all areas of their lives (pervasive). Optimists did just the opposite. If they blamed themselves, they weren't overly critical. Often they saw hard times as being externally caused (bad luck or someone else's doing), and they saw the negative effects as being temporary and limited to a specific area of their lives.

When problems crop up in your marriage, seeing them as permanent ("He'll never change") or pervasive ("How can I be happy about other things when I'm unhappy in my marriage?") and not having a balanced view of responsibility ("It's all my fault" or "It's all his fault") will keep you at a disadvantage.

Can you change a fatalistic pessimism into a take-charge optimism? I'm positive you can!

What to Do

Dispute your negative thinking using the mnemonic A-E-I-O-U:

   A. *Alternative* ways to interpret events. ("My husband hardly notices me when he comes home from work. Is he being inconsiderate of my needs *or is he preoccupied with some problem?*") Come up with as many possible alternatives to negative interpretations. Don't automatically believe the worst.

   E. *Evidence* to the contrary. Look for evidence that would point to the negative effects as being temporary and restricted, not permanent and pervasive. Example: change "She never appreciates what I do" to "She has appreciated me many times before."

   I. *Importance and Implications.* How important is this really?

Yes, a marriage is very important, but are you making the problem more dire than it is? And even if you are correct about an interpretation (your husband *is* avoiding you and unhappy with you), what are the implications? Be realistic; it is not the end of the world, and potential solutions do exist.

O. *Overdone* language. Avoid catastrophic words. Is your situation truly *terrible* or is it just difficult? Avoid absolutistic words such as "always" or "never." ("We'll always be in debt. We'll never be able to afford a house.")

U. *Usefulness* of your interpretation. How useful is it to think the way you do? Does it help you make progress or does it slow you down? Some problems do take longer to resolve than others, but if emphasizing that makes you depressed, you're not helping the situation.

List all of your pessimistic beliefs on index cards, followed by some optimistic "challenges" to those beliefs. For example, on card one you may write:

PESSIMISTIC: I have to learn to accept that my marriage will never be better than it already is.

Did You Know . . .

. . . that one way to feel a little better about your spouse (and the economy, your job, and your future) is to watch a happy movie? Researcher Gordon Bower interviewed movie-goers after they watched a sad or a happy movie. People who viewed the happy movie not only felt happier but were more positive about their marriage and their overall life situation. People who viewed the sad movie were not as positive in their opinions.*

While movie-watching is not a remedy for a troubled marriage, the research underscores the point that people do tend to interpret events in light of their current moods. So, if you are unhappy, be careful how you interpret your spouse's behaviors. You may be much more critical than is called for

* McCarthy, Kathleen. Moods—good and bad—color all aspects of life. *APA Monitor*, August, 1991, p.13.

OPTIMISTIC: No problem is permanent. The kinds of new ideas and skills that have helped others can help us, too.

PESSIMISTIC: My parents' marriage failed and now my marriage has problems. I'm doomed to have a failed marriage, too.

OPTIMISTIC: Problems don't make or break a troubled marriage—but my *reaction* to a problem can make a positive difference. I can make choices my parents didn't make.

Review the cards at least ten times a day. This is important. You won't change a pessimistic attitude overnight. By regularly reviewing and challenging negative attitudes, you'll start to think more optimistically.

Keep a list of the specific ways you think your marriage is at least average, if not better than most. (Research shows that if you view your relationship as better than most, you'll persist at problem solving.[4]) You may not like your spouse's way of disciplining the children, but is she a devoted mother? a considerate person? able to negotiate with you? financially responsible? When problems arise, pessimists lose sight of what's strong about a relationship, which undermines their faith and hope.

Keep in Mind

- If you blame yourself, evaluate your partner's role in the marriage, too. Partners may not be equally at fault, but rarely is it entirely one person's fault.

- It's not the situation per se that is causing you trouble; it is your interpretation of the situation.

- You may not have a marriage problem but a thinking problem.

- Believing often makes it so.

Counting Your Blessings

We say "Thank you" when a stranger holds a door open for us, but how often do we thank our mates for the many sacrifices they make? Not very often.

One common reason we don't is that we take our partner's kindnesses for granted. After a while we *expect* our partner to behave in certain helpful ways and only take notice when he or she fails to deliver. Diminished appreciation often happens to us on the job, but at least there we get paid. At home the only currency exchange is how you and your mate express your feelings about each other, and gratitude is an often-overlooked commodity.

Myths of Gratitude

It's easier to say "Thanks" when you're feeling good about your marriage. It's harder when you're dissatisfied. But gratitude, and its expression, is not just a *reflection* of a happy marriage; it is one of the causes. Expressing gratitude makes your spouse feel appreciated and respected, which can only strengthen the quality of the relationship. The failure to express gratitude can be forgiven from time to time, but not routinely. Husbands and wives need to feel they are important to their mates, that they make a difference in each other's lives. Gratitude is one good way of acknowledging the value of your spouse.

"But if I said 'Thank you' all the time to my wife it would sound phony," one man told me. "I think that by not saying it all the time, it means more to her when I finally do say it."

Myth #1:

Showing gratitude too often is too much. Gratitude really is one form of love, and there can never be too much love. Also, it's unlikely that anybody would express thanks *all the time*. (It is the uncommon couple that shows too much gratitude.) If a rare compliment is well received by a spouse, that doesn't necessarily mean she feels more appreciated. She may instead simply feel relieved to learn that she isn't as unappreciated as she was beginning to believe.

Myth #2:

Any appreciation that is coaxed or prodded must be less sincere than that which is expressed spontaneously.

"Well dear, what do you think?"

"About what?"

"About what? About everything! I just finished decorating the cake, I've set the table—and had to scrounge around for that centerpiece your mother gave us last year—the hors d'oeuvres are ready, and *your* family is about to arrive."

"Oh. Yeah, it looks great, it really does. By the way, have you seen the remote control switch? I can't find it anywhere."

What a guy. In this case it's possible he wasn't as appreciative as he could have been. But very often, people do have to be coaxed to express gratitude and it doesn't mean they are any less sincere. *Feeling* grateful and *expressing* it are two different things, particularly if one of you is someone who doesn't express feelings very often. A good rule of thumb to remember is, *if you request compliments or appreciation, don't criticize the feedback as insincere.*

Myth #3:

You can't be grateful and angry at the same time. Of course you can. But when you're angry it requires more effort to acknowledge that which you are grateful for. Many spouses ignore the good qualities of their mate when they feel angry. That only fuels their anger, because their perspective is negatively biased.

On the last day of vacation, Jim wanted to play a round of golf. Hilary had no problem with that, except she wanted him to postpone his outing until the kids were ready to take their afternoon nap. Jim got angry, not just because he wanted to play golf earlier in the day but because he didn't feel Hilary had appreciated that he'd been willing to cut their vacation short so she could attend a family reunion. But in fact,

Hilary had felt so guilty about the short vacation that she did her best to make Jim's vacation "hassle free." So when he griped about postponing his golf game, Hilary got annoyed. Doesn't he appreciate all the sacrifices I've made for him on this trip? she wondered. A little gratitude early on would have gone a long way for this couple. But it wasn't too late to express gratitude even though they were angry with one another, too. And doing so would help each one to feel more appreciated and increase the odds they could work out their differences with no animosity.

Myth #4:

You can only be grateful for positive, not negative, actions. When your spouse hurts you, it's normal to feel sad or angry—certainly not grateful. But many couples will tell you that their troubling times together—however painful—were the catalyst for important changes for which they are now grateful. It's helpful sometimes to look beyond your immediate problems and ask, "Is it possible that something positive could come from this?" Think back on the times of your life when you grew psychologically. Chances are those were difficult times. One of the key attitudes of happy couples is the belief that when problems arise in the relationship, they'll be able to resolve them. (Unfortunately, the only way to nourish such a belief is to experience problems first.)

Expressing gratitude is one of the least complicated and most helpful things you can do to make your marriage more happy and satisfying. Try it. You'll like it!

What to Do

Right before you go to sleep, tell your mate one thing about her (or him) that you are grateful for. You can even select something she said or did that day—something minor, something you might easily have taken for granted—and tell her how much it means to you that she does those things. (This task requires that you spend time thinking about your mate's positive qualities.) It's simple, and it's a nice way to say goodnight.

Compliment your partner. Women tend to be more self-critical than men, so affirmation by their husbands is important and well received.

If it helps to have some structure, choose from among the following categories: appearance, attitude, values, personal habits, social behavior, speech, and skills. An additional two compliments a week (more than you already provide) isn't a lot and can make a difference.

Keep in Mind

- Regular expressions of gratitude diminish the likelihood of taking one another for granted.

- Expressing gratitude encourages your mate to feel grateful, too.

- You can feel grateful and ungrateful at the same time. So if you wish to be understood, it's a good idea to express both sides of your feelings.

- When your mate feels unappreciated, arguments and stubbornness may result. Expressing gratitude is a surefire way to improve cooperation and your partner's mood.

- Think twice about showing your gratitude with expensive gifts. Extravagance is not necessary and sometimes is a reflection of insecurity. Small, symbolic gifts can be appropriate, but a sincere "Thank you" and a warm embrace is all that's usually required.

Secret #30

Regular Progress Checks

You have two choices: you can wait until a problem develops and then try to fix it, or you can try to prevent so many problems from occurring in the first place. If you wait until a problem develops, you run a greater risk for complications. Some problems (such as a discovered affair and the underlying difficulties that prompted the affair) are not easily or quickly resolved. They can leave scars. And even those problems that can be resolved more quickly by using the techniques offered in this book require two forms of commitment: a commitment to initiate necessary changes, and a commitment to adhere to those changes. *Failure to adhere is a major obstacle to successful change.* Research tells us that without some kind of follow-up plan, 50 percent of couples who've successfully made changes in their relationship eventually relapse.[1]

You may follow the old adage, "If it ain't broke, don't fix it." But when it comes to marriage, regular check-ups and tune-ups—even when all is going well—may mean the difference between dissatisfaction and happiness.

What Is a Relapse?

"Things went much better the first week, but last Monday we couldn't have a conversation without getting into an argument. It seems like we're back to square one."

Backsliding is not a relapse. But being discouraged about a backslide may prompt you to abandon your efforts—and that will almost surely result in a relapse.

In chapter 1 I discussed the "Thirty Day Rule." It's helpful to make a sincere effort at improvement for at least thirty days before you evaluate the effectiveness of the techniques. After thirty days, if there has been improvement, keep at it. The only changes you will trust are those that persist over time. But to insure that the changes will persist, you must keep at them.

A common phenomenon in psychotherapy is for a couple to resume their bad habits just when it appears that the positive changes they made might become permanent. One reason for this is that partners sometimes doubt that any changes made will be lasting and they fear getting hurt again. "Can I really trust him this time?" is a sentiment that induces a spouse to back off from cooperative behavior-change efforts and inspires a "wait-and-see" attitude. But without both partners doing their fair share of the changing (even if one's role is only to show encouragement and appreciation for a partner's changes), interactions in the relationship will resemble the old, unsatisfying patterns.

You can't make a sincere effort to bring about change in your relationship while protecting yourself from getting hurt all over again.

What to Do

Predict some of the upcoming external *stressors that might throw you off track.*[2] A new baby means more stress and probably less money to spend frivolously. A change in a child's school schedule or extra-curricular activities may require a shift in a parent's work or leisure schedule. Holidays approaching? The hassles associated with some holidays are legion. Planning on moving? Buying a bigger house? Expect life to be more stressful for the next six months at least. Unhappy with your job or with an upcoming job-related project? Any surgeries on the horizon? Going on a diet? Quitting cigarettes? Reviewing some of the exercises and techniques that worked before (booster sessions) is a good idea. Also, planning special time for the two of you during those predictable, stressful times may be required so you don't lose sight of the marital needs.

Have regularly planned marriage meetings.[3] Schedule them at times you won't be interrupted. The agenda should always include a discussion of what is working in the marriage and plans for fun mutual leisure time. A discussion on what needs improving in the marriage is best handled by stating what each of you is willing to do to make the improvements happen.

Marriage meetings not only may prevent some problems (or nip some others in the bud), they are necessary for couples who've embarked on a marriage improvement program. Without booster sessions and follow-ups, any improvement program runs a greater risk of relapse and failure. By the way, such meetings need not be deadly serious affairs. Take a stroll while talking or enjoy a dish of ice cream together.

Since setbacks are likely, respond to them by asking, "What is the first thing I could do—right now—that would help put us back on track?" Your response to a setback, more than the setback itself, is vital to the success or failure of your improvement efforts. Reacting to a backslide with an attitude of "Why bother trying anymore?" will practically insure failure.

Schedule a relapse and practice recovering successfully from it. Often, some negative behaviors seem out of our control. "It just happened . . . I didn't want to say what I said . . ." One powerful way of gaining control is to *purposely* engage in them and then rehearse a constructive way to "recover." So schedule an argument where you each interrupt and get defensive. Be impolite or critical. Flirt. Do whatever it is that has been a problem for the relationship. As silly as it sounds, this exercise improves the odds that any setback will be minor and temporary.

Keep in Mind

- When a troubling behavior occurs, check to see if the overall trend of change has been positive. If you are used to arguments occurring several times a week, reducing them to once or twice a week represents progress. Keep up the good work.

- How you respond to a setback more powerfully affects your commitment to improvement than does the setback itself.

- Don't expect changes to be made quickly or easily, especially if the problems have been longstanding.

- Don't take any positive changes for granted. Appreciation and encouragement are the yeast to make your satisfaction rise.

Notes

READ THIS FIRST
[1] Greeley, Andrew. *Faithful Attraction: Discovering Intimacy, Love, and Fidelity In American Marriages.* New York: Tor, 1991
[2] Ibid.
[3] Landi, Ann. Who's happy now? *Self*, August 1991, 89-90, 137. A report on a study conducted by Alex Michalos at the University of Guelph in Ontario, Canada.
[4] Mellman, M., Lazarus, Edward, and Rivlin, Allan. Family time, family values. In David Blankenhorn's, Steven Bayone's and Jean Elshtain's (Eds.) *Rebuilding the Nest: New Commitment to the American Family*, Milwaukee: Family Service America, 1990.
[5] White, Lynn. Determinants of divorce: A review. *Journal of Marriage and the Family*, 1990, 52, 904-912.
[6] Brickman, Philip, Coates, Don, and Janoff-Bulman, R. Lottery winners and accident victims: Is happiness relative? *Journal of Personality and Social Psychology*, 36(8), 1978, 917-927.

Chapter 1: UNDERSTANDING THE UPS AND DOWNS OF CHANGING
[1] Coleman, Paul W. Cease Fire On The Home Front. *Redbook*, August, 1991, p.93-94, 118-119.

Chapter 2: KNOWING HOW TO TALK
[1] Tannen, Deborah. *You Just Don't Understand.* New York, 1990.
[2] Lamke, Leanne K. Marital adjustment among rural couples: the role of expressiveness. *Sex Roles, 21* (9-10), 1989, 579-590.
[3] Noller, Patricia & Fitzpatrick, Mary Anne. Marital communication in the eighties. *Journal of Marriage and The Family, 52,* 1990, 832-843.
[4] Weeks, G. & L'Abate, L. *Paradoxical Psychotherapy: Theory and Practice With Individuals, Couples, and Families.* New York: Bruner/Mazel, 1982.

[5] Rudes, Jim. Interactional letters: a reorganization of couple's communication. *Journal of Marital and Family Therapy*, 1992, *18*(2), 189-192.

Chapter 3: MINIMIZING DEFENSIVENESS

[1] Raush, HL., Barry, WA, Hertel, K., and Swain, MA. *Communication, conflict, and marriage*. San Francisco: Jossey Bass, 1974.

[2] Rusbult, C.E., Verette, J., Whitney, G., Slovik, L., and Lipkin, I. Accommodation processes in close relationships: theory and preliminary empirical evidence. *Journal of Personality and Social Psychology*, 1991, *60*(1), 53-78.

[3] Gottman, John. Predicting the longitudinal course of marriages. *Journal of Marital and Family Therapy*, *17*(1), 1991, 3-7.

[4] Schacter, J. & O'Leary, K. Affective intent and impact in marital communication. *American Journal of Family Therapy*, *13*(4), 1985, 17-23.

[5] That exercise inspired by research discussed by Howard Markman in PREP:Preventing Marital Distress Through Constructive Arguing. *Workshop presented at Annual Convention of the American Association for Marriage and Family Therapy, Dallas, 1991.*

[6] Viscott, David. *I Love You, Let's Work It Out*. New York: Simon & Schuster, 1987, p.60

Chapter 4: KNOWING THE BEST WAY TO READ MINDS

[1] Nisbett, RE. & Ross, LD. *Human Inference: Strategies And Shortcomings of Social Judgment*. Englewood Cliffs, New Jersey: Prentice Hall, 1980.

[2] Gottman, John. *Marital Interactions: Experimental Investigations*. New York: Academic Press, 1979.

Chapter 5: PUTTING YOURSELF IN YOUR PARTNER'S SHOES

[1] Nichols, Michael. *The Self In The System*, New York: Brunner/Mazel, 1987.

[2] Smalley, Gary. *Hidden Keys To Loving Relationships*. Audiotape seminar published by Relationships Today, 1988.

Chapter 6: LOWERING EXPECTATIONS (WHEN IT COMES TO RAISING KIDS)

[1] Glenn, N. & McLanahan, S. Children and marital happiness: a further specification of relationships. *Journal of Marriage and the Family*, *44*, 1982, 63-72.

[2] Cowan, C., Cowan, P., Heming, G., Garrett, E. Coysh, W., Curtis-Boles, H., and Curtis-Boles, A. Transitions to parenthood: His, hers, and theirs. *Journal of Family Issues*, *6*, 1985, 451-482.

[3] White, L., Booth, A. and Edwards, J. Children and marital happiness: why the negative correlation? *Journal of Family Issues*, 7, 1986, 131-147.

[4] Baumeister, Roy. *Meanings of Life*. New York: Guilford, 1991, p. 166.

[5] Ibid.

[6] Ibid, p. 163.

[7] Ibid., p.300-301.

[8] Westman, Alida. Do people's presence more than their presents make children happy? *Perceptual and Motor Skills*, 71(2), 1990, 674.

[9] Fincham, F. and Bradbury, T. *The Psychology of Marriage*. New York: Guilford, 1991.

Chapter 7: BALANCING LOGIC AND EMOTION

[1] Sullaway, Megan & Christensen, Andrew. Assessment of dysfunctional interaction patterns in couples. *Journal of Marriage and the Family*, 1983, *45*, 653-660.

[2] Inspired by Luecke, David L. *Prescription For Marriage*. Columbia, Maryland: The Relationship Institute, 1989.

Chapter 8: NOT ALWAYS COMPROMISING

[1] Wile, Daniel B. *Couples Therapy: A Non-Traditional Approach*. New York: John Wiley & Sons, 1981.

[2] Gottman, J. M. & Krokoff, L.J. Marital interaction and marital satisfaction: a longitudinal view. *Journal of Consulting and Clinical Psychology*, *57*, 47-52.

Chapter 9: NOT WITHDRAWING FROM CONFLICT OR CONVERSATION

[1] Gottman, J. M. & Krokoff, L.J. Marital interaction and marital satisfaction: a longitudinal view. *Journal of Consulting and Clinical Psychology*, *57*, 47-52.

[2] Lynch, James. The Broken heart: The psychobiology of human contact. In Robert Ornstein's and Charles Swencionis's *The Healing Brain*. New York: Guilford Press, 1990.

[3] Siegman, A.W., Anderson, R.A., & Berger, T. The angry voice: its effects in the experience of anger and cardiovascular reactivity. *Psychosomatic Medicine*, *52*, 1990, 631-643.

Chapter 10: ENJOYING TIME TOGETHER

[1] Smith, G., Snyder, D., Trull, T., & Monsma, B. Predicting relationship satisfaction from couples use of leisure time. *American Journal of Family Therapy*, 1988, *16*(1), 3-13.

[2] White, Lynn. Determinants of spousal interactions: marital structure or marital happiness. *Journal of Marriage and the Family, 45*(3), 1983, 511-520.

[3] Larson, J., Crane, R., & Smith, C. Morning and night couples: The effect of wake and sleep patterns on marital adjustment. *Journal of Marital and Family Therapy, 17*(1), 1991, 53-65.

[4] Cameron-Bandler, Leslie. *Solutions: Practical and Effective Antidotes for Sexual and Relationship Problems.* San Rafael, CA: Future Pace, Inc., 1985

[5] Larson, J., Crane, R., & Smith, C. Morning and night couples: The effect of wake and sleep patterns on marital adjustment. *Journal of Marital and Family Therapy, 17*(1), 1991, 53-65.

[6] Larson, Bruce. *There's A Lot More To Health Than Not Being Sick.* Garden Grove, CA: Cathedral Press, 1991.

Chapter 11: EFFECTIVE PROBLEM SOLVING
[1] Beach, S.R., Sandeen, E.E., & O'Leary, K.D. *Depression In Marriage.* New York: Guilford, 1990, p.170

[2] O'Hanlon, W. & Weiner-Davis, M. *In Search of Solutions: A New Direction In Psychotherapy.* New York: Norton, 1989.

[3] Weiner-Davis, M. *Divorce Busting.* New York: Summit Books, 1992, p.155.

Chapter 13: HALTING ARGUMENTS THE RIGHT WAY
[1] Halford, W.K., Hahlweg, K., & Dunne, M. The cross-cultural consistency of marital communication associated with marital distress. *Journal of Marriage and the Family, 52*, 1990, 487-500.

[2] Piercy, F. A game for interrupting coercive marital interactions. *Journal of Marriage and Family Therapy, 9*(4), 1983, 435.

Chapter 14: A SPECIAL WAY OF CARING
[1] Jacobson, N.S., Follette, V., & McDonald, D. Reactivity to positive and negative behavior in distressed and nondistressed married couples. *Journal of Consulting and Clinical Psychology*, 1982, *50*, 706-714.

[2] Gottman, John. *Marital Interactions: Experimental Investigations.* New York: Academic Press, 1979.

[3] Gottman, John. Predicting the longitudinal course of marriages. *Journal of Marital and Family Therapy, 17*(1), 1991, 3-7.

[4] Nagler, William *The Dirty Half-Dozen: Six Radical Rules To Make Relationships Last.* New York: Warner, 1991.

[5] Follette, V. M. & Jacobsen, N. S. Treating communication problems from a behavioral perspective. In R. Chosin's, H. Grunebaum's, and M. Herzig's (Eds.) *One Couple, Four Realities: Multiple Perspectives on Couple Therapy,* New York: Guilford, 1990, 249-258.

[6] Stuart, R.B. *Helping Couples Change: A Social Learning Approach to Marital Therapy.* New York: Guilford, 1980

[7] Gottman, J., Notarius, C., Gonso, J., & Markman, H. *A Couple's Guide To Communication.* Champaign, Illinois: Research Press, 1976.

[8] Bader, E. & Peterson, P. *In Quest of the Mythical Mate.* New York: Brunner/Mazel, 1988.

Chapter 15: A COMMITTED RELATIONSHIP

[1] Lauer, J. & Lauer, R. Marriages made to last. *Psychology Today,* June 1985, p.25.

[2] Beach, S.R., Sandeen, E.E., & O'Leary, K.D. *Depression In Marriage.* New York: Guilford, 1990, p.172

Chapter 16: RECOGNIZING YOUR ROLE IN A PROBLEM

[1] Johnson, S. & Greenberg, L. Relating process to outcome in marital therapy. *Journal of Marriage and Family Therapy, 14*(2), 1988, 175-183.

[2] Driscoll, Richard. *The Binds That Tie.* Lexington, MA: Lexington Books, 1991.

[3] Wile, Daniel. *After The Honeymoon: How Conflicts Can Improve Your Relationship.* New York: WIley, 1988, p.200.

[4] O'Hanlon, W. & Weiner-Davis, M. *In Search of Solutions: A New Direction In Psychotherapy.* New York: Norton, 1989.

Chapter 17: BALANCING CAREER AND FAMILY ROLES

[1] Ross, C.E., Mirowsky, J., and Huber, J. Dividing work, sharing work, and in between: marriage patterns and depression. *American Sociological Review,* 1983, *48,* 809-823.

[2] Kessler, R.C. & McRae, J.A. Effect of wives employment on the mental health of married men and women. *American Sociological Review,* 1982, *47,* 216-227.

[3] Biernat, Monica & Wortman, Camille. Sharing of home responsibilities between professionally employed wives and their husbands. *Journal of Personality and Social Psychology,* 1991, *60*(6), 844-860.

[4] White, L. and Keith, B. The effect of shift work on the quality and stability of marital relationships. *Journal of Marriage and the Family,* 1990, *52,* 453-462.

[5] Greeley, Andrew. *Faithful Attraction: Discovering Intimacy, Love, and Fidelity in American Marriages.* New York: Tor, 1991

[6] Merriam, S. & Clark, M. *Lifelines: Patterns of work, love, and learning in adulthood.* San Francisco: Jossey-Bass, 1991.

[7] Barnett, R.C. & Baruch, G. Social roles, gender, and psychological distress. In R. Barnett, L.Beiner, and G. Baruch (Eds.) *Gender & Stress.* New York: The Free Press, 1987.

[8] Etaugh, C. & Poertner, P. Effects of occupational prestige, employment status, and marital status on perceptions of mothers. *Sex Roles, 24*(5-6), 1991, 345-354.

[9] Fincham, F. and Bradbury, T. *The Psychology of Marriage.* New York: Guilford, 1991.

Chapter 18: KNOWING YOU CAN TRUST

[1] Viscott, David. *I Love You, Let's Work It Out.* New York: Simon & Schuster, 1987, p.115.

[2] Weeks, G. & L'Abate, L. *Paradoxical Psychotherapy: Theory and Practice with Individuals, Couples, and Families.* New York: Brunner/Mazel, 1982.

Chapter 19: UNCOVERING HIDDEN AGENDAS

[1] Gottman, J., Notarius, C., Gonso, J., & Markman, H. *A Couples Guide To Communication.* Champaign, Illinois: Research Press, 1976.

Chapter 20: REMAINING CONNECTED TO YOUR ORIGINAL FAMILY

[1] Nichols, Michael. *No Place To Hide: Facing Shame So We Can Find Self-Respect.* New York: Simon & Schuster, 1991.

[2] Friedman, Edwin H. *Generation To Generation: Family Therapy in Church and Synagogue.* New York: Guilford, 1985.

Chapter 21: TAKING TIME FOR YOURSELF

[1] Hudson, Frederic M. *The Adult Years: Mastering The Art of Self-Renewal.* San Francisco: Jossey-Bass, 1991, p.xi

[2] Ibid, p.73.

Chapter 22: KNOWING WHEN TO KEEP QUIET—AND WHEN NOT TO

[1] Prather, Hugh & Prather, Gayle. *A Book for Couples.* New York: Doubleday, 1988, p. 115.

Chapter 23: LOVING IT UP WITH SEX AND AFFECTION

[1] Greeley, Andrew. *Faithful Attraction: Discovering Intimacy, Love, and Fidelity in American Marriages*. New York: Tor, 1991, p. 119-120.

[2] Ibid., p. 210

[3] Frank, E., Anderson, C., and Rubinstein, D. Frequency of sexual dysfunction in "normal" couples. *New England Journal of Medicine*, (July 20, 1978), *299*, 111-115.

[4] Dyrenforth, S. Wooley, & Wooley, S. A woman's body in a man's world: review of findings on body image and weight control. In J.R. Kaplan (Ed.) *A Woman's Conflict: The Special Relationship Between Women and Food*. New Jersey: Prentice-Hall, 1980.

[5] Cash, T. & Pruzinsky, T. (Eds.) *Body Images: Development, Deviance, and Change*. New York: Guilford, 1990, pp. 60-61.

[6] Ibid., p. 64.

[7] Blakeslee, Sandra. Bald facts about male self-esteem. *American Health*, September, 1991, p. 24.

[8] Nerem, R., Levesque, M., & Cornhill, J. Social environment as a factor in diet-induced atherosclerosis. *Science*, *208*, June 27, 1980, p. 1475-1476.

[9] Rudes, Jim. Interactional letters: a reorganization of couple's communication. *Journal of Marital and Family Therapy*, 1992, *18*(2), 189-192.

[10] Barbach, L. & Geinsinger, D. *Going The Distance: Secrets to Lifelong Love*. New York: Doubleday, 1991.

Chapter 24: KEEPING IT BETWEEN THE TWO OF YOU

[1] Kerr, Michael & Bowen, Murray. *Family Evaluation*. New York: W.W. Norton & Co., 1988, p.134-162.

Chapter 25: SPIRITUAL BELIEFS AND SHARED VALUES

[1] Greeley, Andrew. *Faithful Attraction: Discovering Intimacy, Love, and Fidelity in American Marriage*. New York: Tor Books, 1991, p.190.

[2] Thomas, D. & Cornwall, M. Religion and family in the 1980's: discovery and development. *Journal of Marriage and the Family*, *52*, 1990, 983-992.

[3] Freedman, J.L. *Happy People*. New York: Harcourt Brace Jovanovich, 1978.

[4] Zika, S. & Chamberlain, K. Relationship of hassles and personality to subjective well-being. *Journal of Personality and Social Psychology*, *53*(1), 1987, 155-162.

[5] Heath, Douglas. *Fulfilling Lives: Paths to Maturity and Success*. San Francisco: Jossey-Bass, 1991, p.238-239.

[6] Glenn, Norval. Inter-religious marriages in the U.S.: patterns and recent trends. *Journal of Marriage and the Family, 44*(3), 1982, 555-568.

[7] Greeley, Andrew, p.193.

[8] Ibid., p.198.

Chapter 26: HOLDING HANDS DURING ADVERSITY

[1] Bergman, Joel. On odd days and on even days: rituals used in strategic therapy. In L. Wolberg's & M. Araonson's (Eds.) *Group and Family Therapy*, New York: Brunner/Mazel, 1983, 273-281.

[2] Coleman, Paul W. Optimism. *Hudson Valley Magazine*, March, 1992, p.35.

Chapter 27: KNOWING HOW (AND WHEN) TO FORGIVE

[1] Coleman, Paul W. *The Forgiving Marriage: Overcoming Anger And Resentment and Rediscovering Each Other*. Chicago: Contemporary Books, 1989.

[2] Ibid., p.163-179.

Chapter 28: BEING POSITIVELY OPTIMISTIC

[1] Kanner, A.D, Coyne, J.C., & Schaefer, C. Comparison of two modes of stress measurement: daily hassles and uplifts vs. major life events. *Journal of Behavioral Medicine, 4*, 1981, 1-39.

[2] Beavers, R. *Successful Marriage: A Family Systems Approach To Couples Therapy*. New York: Norton, 1985, p.72.

[3] Seligman, Martin E. P. *Learned Optimism*. New York: Knopf, 1991.

[4] Sabourin, S., Laporte, L., & Wright, J. Problem solving, self-appraisal, and coping efforts in distressed and nondistressed couples. *Journal of Marriage and Family Therapy, 16*(1), 1990, 89-97.

Chapter 30: REGULAR PROGRESS CHECKS

[1] Jacobson, N.S., Schmaling, K.B., & Holtzworth-Munroe, A. Component analysis of behavioral marital therapy: Two year follow-up and prediction of relapse. *Journal of Marital and Family Therapy, 13*, 187-195.

[2] Carlson, J., Sperry, L., & Dinkmeyer, D. Marriage maintenance: How to stay healthy. *Topics In Family Psychology and Counseling, 1*(1), 1992, 84-90.

[3] Ibid., p.88

Troubleshooter's Index

Do you have a specific problem or concern in your marriage? This Troubleshooter's Index* lists the more common concerns of couples and which intervention you may wish to try first.

PROBLEM/ISSUE	WHAT TO DO
Too *accusatory*	Make A-B-C statements (page 28)
	Don't ask "Why?" questions (page 29)
Can't *agree*	Check for hidden agendas (page 107)
	Rehearse problem-solving steps from chapter 11.
	Toss a coin (page 68)
	Change context of discussion (page 30)
Too *angry*; temper flare-ups	Speak slowly and softly (page 54)
	Apologize; call a time-out to calm down (page 54)
Repetitive *arguments*	Try reflective listening (page 23)
	Check for emotional triangles (page 136)
Puzzled how discussions turn into *arguments*	Tape your discussions (page 75)

* The idea for this index was obtained from the book *A Couple's Guide to Communication* by John Gottman, Cliff Notarius, Jonnie Gonso, and Howard Markman. Champaign, IL: Research Press, 1976.

Don't feel *appreciated*	Do gratitude exercises (page 163)
Must question spouse about events concerning *betrayal*	Schedule the dialogue, keep it time-limited (page 102)
Too much *blaming*	Practice relabeling (page 90) Write out concerns in letter (page 29)
Bringing up the past	Hidden agendas (page 107)
Need more *caring*	Do "caring days (page 79)
Feel *caught in the middle*	Check for emotional triangles (page 136)
Less sure of own *commitment*	Act "as if" (page 85)
Spouse less *committed* than you	Don't badger or pursue. Admit concerns but concentrate on other (non-marital) fulfilling activities (page 85)
Can't make a point without *complaining*	Preface your remarks (page 28) Write out concern (page 29)
You feel you *compromise* too much	Reduce hidden compromises (page 48)
Spouse *compromises* too little	Hidden agendas (page 107)
Spouse sees you as *critical*	Do "intent-impact" cards (page 28)
Spouse getting too *defensive*	Admit you must not understand something and ask spouse for clarification (page 29)
sexual desire needs a boost	Talk more, show affection more. Make love without reaching orgasm (page 130)

	Write an "unpredictable" love letter (page 131)
Feel *distant* from spouse	Show affection eight to ten times a day (page 129)
Need more *empathy*	Emotional word-pictures (page 37)
Raising children in an inter-*faith* marriage	Don't allow differences in dogma to detract from role as a parent (page 142)
Unsure you can *forgive*	"I forgive you" task (page 153)
Mate *forgiven* you but still expresses anger	Don't criticize. Try "I forgive you" exercise (page 153)
No *fun*	Increase fun activities (page 59) Brainstorm (page 59)
Marital *goals* hard to achieve	Make goals specific (page 18) Look for hidden agendas (page 107) Look for "marriage-go-rounds" (page 88-89)
Want to measure your level of marital *happiness*	Use formula in chapter 23.
Impatient and complaining that spouse not changing quickly enough	Rate performance daily without discussion (page 18) Follow "thirty day rule" (page 17)
Insults	A-B-C statements (page 28) Intent-impact cards (page 28)
Spouse *interrupts*	Have one-sided conversations (page 23)
Jumping to conclusions	Relabeling (page 90)

	A-B-C statements (page 28)
Spouse too *logical* and unfeeling	Don't get overemotional. Talk on both a logical and a feeling level (page 45)
Not enough *leisure* with mate	"Make the mundane special" (page 58)
One of you is the main initiator of *leisure* activities	Make a "creative list" (page 59)
	Take turns initiating (page 59)
Poor *listening*	Reflective listening (page 23)
Mindreading	Preface mindreading remarks (page 33)
One is a *morning person* and other is a *night person*	Make minor adjustments to your sleep-wake schedule (page 60)
Frustrated with your job as a *parent*	Emphasize positive things you've done as a parent (page 42)
One spouse feels *put down*	Practice validation (page 24)
Pessimistic attitude	Do A-E-I-O-U task (page 157-158)
Feel unskilled at *problem-solving*	What contributed to successful problem-solving in the past? (page 67)
Spouse *pushes your buttons*	Do "seven pennies" task (page 75)
Spouse preoccupied but *refuses to talk*	Encourage talking without being pushy or demanding (page 146)
Too many *role demands* leave you tired and unhappy	Add some small but positive events to your day (page 41)
Rude and inconsiderate	Do a "politeness week" (page 80)
Don't feel *special*	Do "special day" task (page 48-49)

Stubborn standoffs Can't *talk* without *arguing*	Hidden agendas (page 107)
Afraid changes made will be *temporary*	Follow "thirty day rule" (page 17) Do regular progress checks (chapter 30)
Tit-for-tat exchanges	Slow down dialogue; practice showing caring toward spouse when spouse does not reciprocate (page 79-80)
Get *uncomfortable* when spouse discloses feelings	Don't offer spouse advice unless explicitly asked (page 24) Do diaphragmatic breathing (page 53)
Spouse makes *unfair* comments	Acknowledge any merit to what's being said before disagreeing (page 24)
Spouse *withdraws* during conflict	Halt name-calling, interruptions, and loud exchanges. Speak more slowly and softly. Rehearse reflective listening (page 23)

Index

A-B-C Statements, 28

A-E-I-O-U, 158

A-E-I-O-U, to overcome pessimism, 157

abusiveness, 12

accepting partner's feelings, 36

acting committed, 85

addiction, 12

admitting blame, 91

adversity, 143, 146, 155

    helping children cope with, 146, 147

    positive affects of, 145

affection, importance of, 129

affection, without sex, 129

alcoholism, 12

annoying behavior in spouse, 124, 125

anticipating difficult conversations, 45

apologizing, 150

appreciating changes, 17, 19

appreciating spouse, importance of, 71, 79

arbitrariness, 68

arguments, effective ending of, 73, 75

balancing reason and emotion, 44

blaming partner for unhappiness, 115

bonding with your spouse, 112

booster sessions, 166

brainstorming, 65
caring, 77, 80, 129
caring days, 79, 80
caring to conflict ratio, importance of, 78
changes in relationship, making, 16, 42, 166
changing your spouse, 91, 92
childless couples, Gallup survey, 40
children, 39, 40
churchgoing, 142
coercion, 74
commitment
    as a bargaining tool, 86
    definition of, 84, 85
    and happiness, 84
    and intimacy, 83
    positive consequences of, 86
    to make change successful, 165
communication, 24, 44, 72, 114, 125, 18, 153, 49, 68,
71, 85, 90, 97, 108
    communicating vs. talking, 21
    expression of feelings, 24
    importance of timing, 126
    improvement, 44
    interrupting, 25
    including a middleman, 138
    physical stance, 53
    problem-solving, 24
    proper breathing, 53
    recognizing issues, 45
    voice style, 54
complaining effectively, 29-30
compromise, 47-49
conflict avoidance, 51-52, 53, 55
conflict, effects of, 51
confrontation, 152

connecting with family, as individuals, 114
conversation, mechanics of, 22
conversation, one-sided, 23
coping, 148
coping, differences in style, 145
creative brainstorming, 59
criticism, 18
dealing with anger, 29-30
defensiveness, 28-30
disconnecting from original family, importance of, 113
discouragement, 70
divorce
    odds increased by age, 11
    rate among dual-career couples, 95
    social acceptability, 11
dual career couples, 94-97
    divorce rate among, 95
    problem-solving techniques, 96
emotional triangles, 133-137
"emotional word-pictures", 37
empathy
    definition of, 35.
    essential ingredients of, 35
    exchanging roles, 38
    in family relationships, 114
empty nest syndrome, 40
encouragement, importance of, 71
expectations, conflicting, 22
expressiveness, emotional, 22, 146
external stressors, 166
faith, importance of, 156, 159
family relationships
    difficulties of family gatherings, 111
    effective family communication, 114
    responding to familial behavior patterns, 114

separating from original family, importance of, 112
setting goals, 113
unresolved family issues, 111
fear of love, 113
forgiveness
    as a decision, 150
    difficulties of, 149
    effective communication, 153
    phases of, 151
    and prayer, 154
"The Forgiving Marriage", 151
goal setting, 18
Grace Scale, 140
gratitude
    importance of, 41, 161
    means of expressing, 163
    myths about, 161, 162, 163
    positive effects of, 164
hidden agendas, 106, 107, 108, 109, 125
hidden compromises, 81
hope, importance of, 156, 159
"I Forgive You" Exercise, 153
impatience, 18
individuality, sense of, 118
Intent-Impact cards, 28
inter-faith marriages, 140
intimacy, 21
introspection, 120
jealousy, 101
job-switching, 42
leisure time, planning, 61
letter writing, 24, 25
listening effectively, 145
lovemaking, scheduling, 130

marital happiness
 decline of, 39
 definition of, 11
 for fathers, 40
 Gallup study, 10
 and likelihood of divorce, 11
 importance of, 10
 monitoring, 130
 relative to age of children, 40
marriage meetings, 166-167
maturity, 112
mind reading, 31, 32, 33, 34, 48
miscommunication, 23
mismatched couples, 58
mistrust, 99-101
morning vs. night partner, 58
mutual support, 70, 143, 144
mutual understanding, 23, 25
negative interactions, 27
non-verbal arguing, 74
non-verbal expressions, 22
non-verbal messages, 22, 25
optimism, 155
optimists, characteristics of, 157
parenthood paradox, 40
parenting, positive value of, 42
pattern of interaction, 27
personal time, importance of, 120
pessimism, 155, 157, 158, 159
physical connections, importance of, 76
politeness week, 80
prayer, 139
problem cycle, 88
problems
 identifying, 12, 105, 106

recurrent, 64, 66
problem-solving
    difficulties of, 63
    evaluating problems, 64
    evaluating progress, 65, 167
    effective communication, 90, 108
    features often overlooked, 66, 67
    four-step approach, 64
    manipulative problem-solving, 89
    setting guidelines, 64
    visualization, 90
    as a skill, 64
reason vs. emotion, 43, 45
reflective listening, 23, 25, 66, 71, 136, 146, 152
religion in marriage, 139, 140, 141, 142
renewal in marriage, 154
repetitive agruments, 81, 105, 107
requesting change, 36
resentment, 48, 49
resolving anger, 115
reviewing conversations, 37
role-playing, 75
secrets, danger of, 115
self-image, importance of, 128
self-neglect, dangers of, 117
self-renewal, 118, 120, 121
selfishness, 117
Seligman, Dr. Martin, 157
setbacks, response to, 167
setting goals, 16
sex
    frequency of, 127
    importance of manner, 129
    visualization, 130
    wives' interest in, 127

sexual satisfaction
    importance of, 127
    and marital satisfaction, 128
    to increase, 131
shared interests and activities, 58, 61
sleep-wake pattern, 60
solitary activities, 41, 61
"Speak Up Hour", 125
special days, 49, 59
spending time together, 57
stonewalling, 52, 53
taking actions for granted, 79
"Thirty Day Rule," 17, 65, 165
Time-Out, 29, 54
transferring blame, 70, 89
trust
    and caring, 81
    importance of, 99, 102, 104
    regaining, 99, 100, 102, 103
understanding, 36, 38, 48
unsatisfying relationships, cause of, 44
validating partner's comments, 24
values, 140
Viscott, David, 101
visualization, 125, 59, 60, 90
willpower, 16